Lion House

Other Lion House Cookbooks

Lion House Cookies and Sweets

Lion House Cakes and Cupcakes

Lion House Pies

Lion House Bakery

Lion House Christmas

Lion House Classics

Lion House Weddings

Compiled by

Brenda Hopkin and David Bench

Salt Lake City, Utah

Photo Credits

Robert Casey—pages 4, 11, 12, 15, 18, 25, 27, 28, 33, 36, 41, 45, 53, 60, 65, 66, 69, 72, 74, 80, 84, 91, 92, 95, 98, 103, 104, 109, 112, 118

John Luke—pages 17, 21, 57, 117, 127

Alan Blakely—pages 47, 79, 87, 123, 130

Maxine Bramwell—Food styling on above

Shauna Gibby—Art direction and photo styling on above

Russell Winegar—page 2; Susan Massey—food stylist

Cover photo: Savory Tomato Basil Bisque (page 77)

Thanks to the Lion House Pantry staff and their families for sharing a few of their favorite family recipes and for preparing and testing many of the recipes in this book as we reduced the recipes from Pantry size to home use.

Visit us at DeseretBook.com

Library of Congress Cataloging-in-Publication Data

Lion House soups and stews / compiled by Brenda Hopkin and David Bench.
pages cm
Includes index.
ISBN 978-1-60907-156-1 (hardbound : alk. paper)
1. Soups. 2. Stews. 3. Cooking—Utah—Salt Lake City. I. Hopkin, Brenda, editor of compilation. II. Bench, David, editor of compilation. III. Lion House (Restaurant)
TX757.L57 2012
641.81'3—dc23 2012016929

Printed in China
R. R. Donnelley, Shenzhen, China

10 9 8 7 6 5 4 3 2 1

CONTENTS

Indicates this recipe may be made in a slow cooker.

INTRODUCTION

From 1856 to the present, the Lion House has been making a wide variety of food for the enjoyment of all those who ever once lived in the Lion House or, currently, for those who visit there.

When Brigham Young's family resided in the Lion House, baking and cooking went on almost around-the-clock. Approximately seventy-five people needed to be fed three meals a day, and there was only one wood-burning stove to cook everything on. Brigham Young's wives became very skilled at turning out the best food of that day.

Today the Lion House Bakery is still turning out the best food of the day almost around-the-clock. The skilled staff takes great pride in providing soups, baked goods, and other hot entrees for fans throughout the world, plus the many new fans who happen to be in the area of one of the Lion House pantries located in a Deseret Book store. Of course they don't use a wood-burning stove anymore, but just as much love goes into the baking of each roll or cookie and preparing each soup as it did in Brigham's day.

Cooking should be enjoyable, and the finished product should reflect your favorite flavors. Soup recipes should be used as guidelines, not barriers, so improvise and have fun. If you like garlic, add an extra clove to your chicken noodle soup. If you don't like peeling potatoes, leave the skins on. Our recipes are your recipes, so feel free to change and adapt and make them the way you want.

There are some fun new recipes in *Lion House Soups and Stews,* plus some recipes from other Lion House cookbooks that are now out of print. The DVD will give you pointers and tips that many seasoned cooks may not be familiar with.

May all who use this book have many hours of enjoyment in making delicious soups and stews or in finding a new skill—one that will enrich your lives and bring a smile to all who partake of your creations. HAPPY COOKING!

Clockwise from top left: Carrot Bisque (page 83), Gazpacho (page 100), Vegetable and Sausage Soup (page 38)

HELPFUL SOUP TIPS

1. Do your preparations (dicing, chopping, and gathering ingredients) before you start cooking so you aren't scrambling to find something while the soup is cooking.
2. When using fresh herbs with small leaves such as parsley or oregano, add the entire stem—leaves and all—to the soup. Cooking will cause the leaves to fall off and the flavor will be imparted to the soup. Remove the large stem before thickening or serving.
3. Noodles and dumplings should be added immediately before the soup will be served. They tend to get soggy if made ahead of time and reheated in a soup.
4. Thickening a soup should be done the day a soup will be used, rather than ahead of time. Unthickened soup makes the soup easier to cool and easier to reheat without scorching.
5. Garnishes add a splash of color, a new texture, or a surprising flavor to an already wonderful soup. They are also a fun way to share a bit of your own style with family and guests. Simple garnishes made from reserved vegetables already in the soup—but cut thin and left crisp—are always a nice garnish. A dollop of sour cream or a drizzle of olive oil will add a color contrast or shine. Fresh herbs or cracked black pepper also enhance the look of a finished soup. Crisp, toasted bread is a simple garnish that adds new texture, whether it is crispy or allowed to soften in the hot soup.
6. Leftover soups should be cooled from 135 degrees down to 40 degrees in less than 4 hours. Thick, heavy soups and stews will not cool quickly enough in a refrigerator. To cool quickly, fill the kitchen sink with ice and water until water covers the sides of the pot but the pot does not float. Stir soup frequently to speed the process. Soups may also be cooled by adding ice directly to the soup. If you make the soup a little thicker than usual, ice may be added and will not affect the final product when reheated.
7. Reheat soup to a minimum of 165 degrees as quickly as possible without burning it. Boiling is not necessary, as it can overcook the ingredients or cause cream soups to curdle.

Figure 1
Figure 2
Figure 3
Figure 4

Beef Stock

Makes 2–3 quarts

5–6 pounds beef soup bones cut into 1-inch pieces by butcher
1 large onion, chopped but unpeeled
3 large carrots, chopped into ½-inch pieces
3 ribs celery, including some leaves, chopped into ½-inch pieces
½ cup water plus water to cover ingredients
1 (6-ounce) can tomato paste
8 peppercorns
6 sprigs fresh parsley with stems
1 bay leaf
1 tablespoon salt
4 sprigs fresh thyme
2 cloves garlic, peeled

Preheat oven to 450 degrees F. Place bones, onion, carrots, and celery in a large, shallow roasting pan (Figure 1). Bake, uncovered, about 30 minutes or until bones are well browned, turning occasionally (Figure 2). Drain off fat.

Place browned ingredients in a large soup pot or Dutch oven. Pour ½ cup water into the roasting pan and stir with a wooden spoon to loosen all the browned bits (Figure 3). Pour this liquid into the soup pot. Add tomato paste, peppercorns, parsley, bay leaf, salt, thyme, and garlic. Add enough cold water to cover ingredients. Bring mixture to a boil (Figure 4). Reduce heat to a low simmer and cook 5 to 6 hours, skimming the top several times with a spoon or fine mesh strainer. Strain stock through a fine mesh strainer into another large stockpot or heatproof container, discarding the solids.

Cool immediately in a large cooler of ice or a sink full of ice water to below 40 degrees F. Refrigerate overnight. Remove and discard solidified fat from surface of liquid. Store stock in a covered container in the refrigerator 2 to 3 days or in the freezer up to 3 months. Use as the base for any broth soup.

Chef's Tip: The smaller the bones are cut, the more flavor the stock will have.

Chicken Stock

Makes 2–3 quarts

- 3–4 pounds chicken carcasses, including necks and backs
- 1 large onion, roughly chopped into large pieces
- 4 carrots, chopped
- 4 ribs celery, chopped
- 10 sprigs fresh thyme
- 10 sprigs fresh parsley with stems
- 2 bay leaves
- 8–10 peppercorns
- 2 whole cloves garlic, peeled
- Water to cover all ingredients

Place chicken, vegetables, herbs, and spices in a large stockpot. Cover ingredients with cold water. Cook on high heat until bubbles break through the surface of the liquid. Turn heat down to medium-low so stock maintains a low, gentle simmer. Skim the top layer from the stock with a spoon or fine mesh strainer three or four times for the first hour of cooking and twice each hour for the next 2 hours. Add hot water as needed to keep bones covered. Simmer, uncovered, 6 to 8 hours.

Strain stock through a fine mesh strainer into another large stockpot or heatproof container, discarding the solids. Cool immediately in a large cooler of ice or a sink full of ice water to below 40 degrees F. Refrigerate overnight. Remove and discard solidified fat from surface of liquid. Store stock in a covered container in the refrigerator 2 to 3 days or in the freezer up to 3 months. Use as the base for any broth soup. Boil 2 minutes, prior to use.

Roux

1 cup flour
½ cup butter (no substitutions)

Roux is the most common thickener for soups and sauces. It is made by combining flour and butter, cooked to form a paste. The butterfat coats the starch granules, preventing them from lumping together when added to liquid. Roux can be prepared in larger batches and stored in the refrigerator for use in many recipes. Different types of roux are used in different recipes, and they vary depending on the amount of time they are cooked and how dark they are.

White roux is cooked only briefly and should be removed from heat as soon as it develops a bubbly appearance. It is used in white sauces and soups when no color is desired.

Blonde roux is cooked just long enough to take on some color as the flour caramelizes. Blonde roux is used the most and has a richer flavor than white roux.

Brown roux is cooked considerably longer than white or blonde roux. It needs to develop a dark color and a rich, nutty aroma and flavor. It is used in brown sauces and dishes where dark color is desired. Because cooking breaks down starches and prevents gelatinization, more brown roux is required to thicken a liquid than blonde roux.

Chef's Tip: Never add hot roux to hot liquid. Cold roux may be added to hot liquid or cold liquid to hot roux, but *never* hot to hot.

White Sauce (Béchamel)

1 recipe Roux (page 7)
1 small onion, finely chopped
1 tablespoon butter
1 cup heavy cream
1 quart milk
¼ teaspoon ground cloves
¼ teaspoon nutmeg, or to taste
Salt and pepper, to taste

Make one recipe of roux. Allow to cool completely in the refrigerator. Sauté onion in butter in a large saucepan until onion is translucent. Add cream, milk, cloves, and nutmeg. Bring to a slow simmering boil. Add 3 tablespoons cold roux to hot liquid and allow to come to a boil, stirring gently. Continue to add roux 2 tablespoons at a time, bringing to a boil and stirring gently after each addition, until sauce reaches desired consistency. Season to taste with salt and pepper. This recipe may be used as a base for soups and sauces, such as with the following:

- Roasted red peppers
- Roasted corn and potatoes
- Baked potato and all your favorite toppings
- Roasted tomatoes
- Roasted root vegetables
- Cauliflower, broccoli, and carrots
- Clams, diced potatoes, crumbled bacon, celery, and thyme
- Zucchini and other garden vegetables you need to use
- Pumpkin or squash pureed with a little nutmeg
- Chopped spinach
- Sautéed mushrooms
- Any cheese for a sauce or soup
- Roasted garlic
- Pesto

Chef's Tip: White sauce may be made ahead and frozen. Allow the sauce to cool a bit and then place 1–2 cup portions in zip-top freezer bags and place in freezer. Thaw by placing unopened bag in a bowl of warm water. Place thawed sauce in a pan and heat over medium heat until warm.

Hearty Chicken Noodle Soup

Makes about 2½ quarts, or 10 (1-cup) servings

- 2 teaspoons paste-style chicken soup base, or 2 bouillon cubes, or 1 teaspoon granulated base
- 3 cups canned or homemade chicken stock
- 2 cups peeled and chopped carrots
- 2 cups chopped celery
- ¾ cup chopped onion
- 2 (10¾-ounce) cans condensed cream of chicken soup
- ¼ cup evaporated milk, or ½ cup milk
- Roux (page 7)
- 2 cups cooked diced chicken
- 4 cups cooked noodles (see Homemade Herb Noodles below)
- Salt and pepper, to taste

Heat chicken soup base and stock together. Add carrots, celery, and onion and simmer until vegetables are crisp-tender. Add cream of chicken soup, milk, cooked chicken, and noodles. Thicken with roux, if needed. Add salt and pepper, to taste.

Homemade Herb Noodles

- 1 cup flour
- 1 teaspoon herb of choice (such as parsley, thyme, basil, oregano, or chives)
- 1 egg
- Water to bind

Combine flour and herb on work surface. Form a cone in flour and work egg into flour. Add water a spoonful at a time to make a firm yet workable dough. Allow dough to rest 15 to 20 minutes. Roll out paper-thin; cut into strips. Allow to dry to store for later use or cook 12 to 16 minutes in 2 quarts salted water until tender, stirring gently. Drain and add noodles to desired soup.

Country-Style Chicken Noodle Soup

Makes 6 servings

½ cup diced yellow onion
1 cup diced celery
1 cup diced carrots
2 tablespoons vegetable oil
1 pound boneless, skinless chicken breast, diced
8 cups chicken broth or stock,* canned or homemade
4 ounces egg noodles, uncooked
Salt and pepper, to taste
1 small bunch parsley, finely chopped, for garnish

Sauté onion, celery, and carrots in oil in a heavy soup pot until onion is translucent; do not let them brown. Add diced chicken and cook until done. Add chicken broth and bring to a boil. Add uncooked noodles. Return to a boil and cook until noodles are done. Add salt and pepper, to taste, and garnish with fresh parsley.

**This soup is best when made with chicken broth. If broth is not available, you may substitute 8 cups water and 8 chicken bouillon cubes. Adjust the flavor with salt.*

Chef's Tip: Alternately, you may use the breast meat of a rotisserie chicken and the juice from its container as part of the stock. Add cut-up chicken after noodles are cooked.

Chicken and Rice Soup

Makes 8 servings

1 (2½–3-pound) fryer chicken
4 cups water
1 peeled carrot, cut in chunks
2 onions, divided (1 cut in chunks for broth, 1 chopped for soup)
1 celery rib, cut in chunks
1 teaspoon salt
1 clove garlic, crushed
1 cup cooked rice
2 fresh tomatoes, cut in wedges
½ cup chopped green pepper
1 cup frozen peas
¼ cup sliced pimiento-stuffed olives

Place chicken, water, carrot, onion chunks, celery, salt, and garlic in a large soup pot. Bring to a slow boil and then reduce heat to simmer. Cover and simmer 1 hour. Remove chicken from broth and set aside to cool slightly. Strain vegetables from broth and discard; set broth aside to cool. Once chicken is cool enough to handle, remove and discard bones and skin. Cut chicken into bite-sized pieces.

Skim fat off the broth and return broth to stove top. Stir in cut-up chicken, rice, tomatoes, green pepper, chopped onion, peas, and olives. Heat, uncovered, until hot and peppers and onion are tender, about 10 minutes.

Southwest Chicken Tortilla Soup

Makes 6 to 8 servings

2 tablespoons melted butter
2 cups diced boneless, skinless chicken breasts
2 teaspoons minced garlic
2 tablespoons diced yellow onion
2 (4-ounce) cans diced green chiles
2 cups tomato puree
1 cup frozen whole kernel corn, thawed
2 cups diced yellow corn tortillas
4 cups water
2 cups heavy cream
½ teaspoon cumin
2 teaspoons salt
½ teaspoon Cajun seasoning
1 diced tomato, for garnish
1 cup sour cream, for garnish
10–16 tortilla chips or 3 cups tortilla strips, for garnish

Melt butter in a soup pot and sauté raw chicken until almost cooked. Add garlic and onion, cooking 4 minutes. Add chiles, tomato puree, corn, tortillas, water, and cream; simmer. Blend with an immersion blender* until smooth. Season with cumin, salt, and Cajun seasoning.

To serve, ladle into serving bowls and garnish with diced tomato, sour cream, and tortilla chips or strips.

**In place of an immersion blender, a regular blender may be used, with caution. Fill the blender about one-third full so that the hot liquid does not splatter over. Vent the lid of the blender so that the steam inside does not build up pressure.*

Slow Cooker: Place all ingredients, except garnishes, in slow cooker. Cook on high 3 to 4 hours. Blend with immersion blender. Add garnishes and serve.

Chicken Dumpling Soup

Makes 12 servings

Dumplings

1 cup milk

½ cup butter

½ teaspoon salt

½ teaspoon nutmeg

1 cup flour

3 eggs

Soup

1 large yellow onion, diced

½ stalk celery, diced

2 carrots, diced

2 tablespoons vegetable oil

Meat from 1 chicken, cooked and shredded

4 to 6 cups chicken broth

1 cup frozen French-cut or fresh cut green beans

1 cup pearl barley, optional

1 teaspoon celery salt

1 tablespoon fresh chopped parsley

2 bay leaves

1 teaspoon thyme

Salt and pepper, to taste

For dumplings: Bring milk and butter to a boil; add salt and nutmeg. Remove from heat and immediately add flour, stirring until dough leaves sides of pan. Add eggs one at a time, forming a sticky dough.

For soup: Sauté onion, celery, and carrots in oil. Add remaining ingredients and simmer until barley is tender and vegetables are softened. Season to taste with salt and pepper. Add spoon-sized balls of dumpling dough (they will sink to the bottom) and simmer until dumplings rise.

Mulligatawny

Makes 10 servings

3½ pounds chicken pieces
6 cups water
1 teaspoon coriander
½ teaspoon turmeric
½ ounce fresh gingerroot, chopped fine
¼ teaspoon cayenne pepper
6 peppercorns, ground
1 teaspoon butter
1 onion, finely chopped
Salt and pepper, to taste
5 cups hot cooked rice

Place the chicken pieces and water in a large saucepan, cover, and boil gently for 20 minutes. Skim off fat. Add coriander, turmeric, ginger, cayenne pepper, and peppercorns; cover and simmer until chicken is tender, about 40 to 50 minutes. Strain broth through a fine sieve into a bowl; set aside. Remove chicken from bones and add to broth. Melt butter in a large frying pan; add onion and sauté until translucent. Stir in broth and chicken. Season to taste with salt and pepper. Simmer 1 hour until slightly thickened. Serve over cooked rice.

Hearty Turkey Vegetable Soup

Makes 8 servings

Turkey Broth

1 roasted turkey
1 small carrot, sliced
1 small onion, chopped
Celery leaves
2 teaspoons salt
1 bay leaf

Soup

8 cups canned turkey broth (or see above)
1 cup cubed potatoes
1 cup sliced carrots
1 cup sliced celery
¼ cup chopped onion
1 teaspoon salt
Pepper, to taste
1 cup uncooked egg noodles
2 cups chopped cooked turkey meat
1 cup frozen peas

For broth: Strip as much meat as possible from bones of roasted turkey; refrigerate meat for later use in soup. Place bones and skin into a large stockpot and barely cover with water. Add carrot, onion, a few celery leaves, salt, and bay leaf. Bring to a simmer over medium heat. Reduce heat, cover, and simmer 2 to 3 hours. Strain broth, discarding carcass and other solids. Use broth immediately or refrigerate and use within 2 days. You may also freeze broth for 3 to 6 months.

For soup: Combine turkey broth, potatoes, carrots, celery, onion, salt, and pepper in a large soup pot. Bring to a boil over medium-high heat. Add noodles, reduce heat, and simmer 30 minutes. Stir in turkey and frozen peas; heat thoroughly and serve.

Mongolian Hot Pot

Makes about 10 cups, or 10 (1-cup) servings

½ pound bacon, diced
1 pound lean ground beef, or 2 cups diced cooked ham
1 (10½-ounce) can condensed beef broth, or 1 tablespoon paste-style beef soup base with ¾ cup water
4 cups water
1 onion, chopped
1 green pepper, chopped
1 carrot, sliced
1 tablespoon soy sauce
1 (14½ -ounce) can diced tomatoes
1 (10–12-ounce) package frozen mixed vegetables
1 zucchini, sliced
2 teaspoons salt
⅛ teaspoon pepper
1 tablespoon finely chopped parsley, for garnish

Fry bacon in large, heavy saucepan until crisp. Pour off all but 2 tablespoons bacon fat. Drain bacon on paper towel. Sauté beef or ham in the 2 tablespoons bacon fat. Add beef broth, water, onion, green pepper, carrot, soy sauce, and tomatoes and simmer gently about 1 hour. Add mixed vegetables and zucchini, and simmer another 10 minutes. Add salt and pepper. Adjust seasonings to taste.

Garnish with chopped parsley just before serving.

Slow Cooker: Fry bacon and sauté beef or ham, as above. Place all ingredients in slow cooker and cook 4 hours on low.

Steak Soup

Makes 4 servings

- 1 large onion, thinly sliced
- 1 tablespoon vegetable oil
- 12 ounces top sirloin steak, cooked and cut into thin strips (leftover steak is fine)
- 3 cups beef broth
- ½ to 1 teaspoon salt
- ¼ teaspoon pepper
- 1 or 2 cloves garlic, minced
- ¼ teaspoon cumin
- ¼ teaspoon paprika
- 2 large potatoes, peeled and cut in strips
- 2 eggs, separated
- ½ cup cream
- 2 sprigs parsley, chopped, for garnish

Sauté onion in oil in a large saucepan. Add steak strips, beef broth, salt, pepper, garlic, cumin, and paprika. Simmer 5 minutes. Add potatoes and simmer until potatoes are tender. Remove from heat. Beat egg whites slightly and add slowly to hot broth, stirring constantly. Blend egg yolks with cream and stir into soup, stirring slightly just to blend.

Garnish with parsley and serve immediately.

Beef and Barley Soup

Makes 10 servings

½ pound lean boneless round steak
9 cups water
1 (14½-ounce) can stewed tomatoes, undrained and diced
1 (10½-ounce) can beef broth
½ cup chopped onion
1 clove garlic, minced
½ teaspoon basil
¼ teaspoon salt
2 bay leaves
½ cup pearl barley
1 (10–12-ounce) package frozen mixed vegetables

Prepare steak by trimming fat and cutting steak into 1-inch cubes. In a large soup pot (at least 4-quart capacity), stir together 8 cups water, steak cubes, tomatoes, broth, onion, garlic, basil, salt, and bay leaves. Bring to a boil. Reduce heat; cover and simmer 1 hour. Place barley in a strainer and rinse with cold water. Gradually add barley, along with 1 cup water, to soup in pot; cover and simmer again 1 hour. Skim fat from top of soup. Add frozen vegetables to soup pot; cover and simmer a third time until meat and vegetables are tender, about 30 to 40 minutes. Remove and discard bay leaves.

Serve with a crostini (see below).

Slow Cooker: Prepare meat and rinse the barley. Place all ingredients, minus 1 cup of water, in the slow cooker. Cook on high 3 to 4 hours.

Crostini

Crostini are a fun, easy accompaniment or garnish for any soup. To make, slice an Italian-style baguette on a 45-degree bias about ¼-inch thick. Brush each piece with melted butter or olive oil and season with a sprinkle of salt or your favorite dry herb. Bake in a 325-degree F. oven until golden brown. Remove from the oven and let stand on the hot pan and continue to dry.

Beef Minestrone

Makes 6 to 8 servings

1 pound ground beef
1 cup diced onion
1 teaspoon minced garlic
1 tablespoon olive oil
1 (29-ounce) can tomato puree
3 cups water
1 teaspoon salt
1 teaspoon Italian seasoning
1 (10–12-ounce) package frozen mixed vegetables (or fresh carrots, peas, zucchini)
½ (12-ounce) package spiral noodles, uncooked
Pepper, to taste
½ cup Asiago cheese, for garnish

Brown ground beef, onion, and garlic in oil in a large soup pot. Add tomato puree, water, salt, and Italian seasoning. Add vegetables and noodles and continue to cook until vegetables are tender and noodles are cooked. Add pepper, to taste.

To serve, garnish with Asiago cheese.

Slow Cooker: Prepare ground beef, onion, and garlic as above. Place all ingredients, except garnish, in slow cooker and cook on high 2 to 3 hours.

Taco Soup

Makes 8 servings

1 pound ground beef
1 cup chopped onion
1 package mild taco seasoning mix
2 cups frozen corn
1 (15-ounce) can kidney beans, drained and rinsed
1 (28-ounce) can stewed tomatoes, undrained
1 (8-ounce) can tomato sauce
2 cups water
Tortilla chips, for garnish
Shredded cheddar or pepper Jack cheese, for garnish

Brown ground beef and onion in a large soup pot; drain off fat. Stir in taco seasoning, corn, kidney beans, stewed tomatoes, tomato sauce, and water. Bring to a simmer over medium heat and simmer 20 to 30 minutes.

Serve topped with tortilla chips and shredded cheese.

Slow Cooker: Brown ground beef and onion in a frying pan. Place all ingredients, except for garnishes, in slow cooker. Cook on high 3 to 4 hours.

Super Hamburger Soup

Makes 12 servings

1½ pounds extra-lean ground beef
2 onions, chopped
4 ribs celery, chopped
1 green bell pepper, chopped
2 (14½-ounce) cans stewed tomatoes, undrained and diced
1 (6-ounce) can tomato paste
4 cups water
4 medium carrots, peeled and sliced
2 large potatoes, peeled and diced
1 (15¼-ounce) can whole kernel corn, undrained
1 (15-ounce) can red kidney beans, undrained
1 (15-ounce) can lima beans or garbanzos, undrained
1½ teaspoons salt
½ teaspoon pepper
2 zucchini, sliced

Cook ground beef, onions, celery, and green pepper in a large soup pot until meat is brown and crumbly and onion is translucent. Drain. Add tomatoes, tomato paste, water, carrots, potatoes, corn, beans, salt, and pepper. Bring to a boil; reduce heat and simmer, covered, about 20 minutes. Add zucchini and cook another 10 to 15 minutes or until vegetables are tender.

Chef's Tip: Experiment with herbs such as basil, marjoram, thyme, and bay leaves for a more flavorful broth.

Vegetable Beef Soup

Makes 3 quarts, about 12 (1-cup) servings

- 1 cup diced tomatoes
- 1½ cups peeled, diced carrots
- 1 cup diced celery
- 1 cup peeled, diced potatoes
- 7 cups water or beef stock, divided
- ¼ cup chopped onion
- 1 tablespoon paste-style beef soup base or 1½ teaspoons granulated soup base
- ½ cup green beans
- ½ pound cooked beef, cut in bite-sized pieces
- 1 cup peas
- Salt and pepper, to taste

Cook together tomatoes, carrots, celery, potatoes, 6 cups water, onion, and beef soup base in a large soup pot until carrots and celery are tender. Add green beans, beef, and 1 cup water. Simmer until vegetables are tender. Add peas about 5 minutes before serving. Adjust seasonings to taste. Serve with Parmesan bread (page 125) or your favorite crackers.

Slow Cooker: Place all ingredients in slow cooker. Cook on high 3 to 4 hours or on low 6 to 8 hours.

Oxtail Soup

Makes 6 to 8 servings

3 pounds oxtail, cut into pieces at the joints
1 cup peeled, chopped carrots
1½ cups chopped onion
1 cup chopped celery
1 tablespoon minced garlic
2 tablespoons butter
1 (12-ounce) can tomato paste
8 cups beef stock, divided
¼ cup chopped parsley
1 teaspoon chopped fresh rosemary
1 bay leaf
4–6 small red potatoes, cut in quarters
Roux, to thicken (page 7)
Salt and freshly ground pepper, to taste

Preheat oven to 400 degrees F. Place oxtail pieces in a roasting pan and put in oven to brown 35 minutes or until dark brown. Turn frequently to avoid burning. Remove pan from oven and discard any fat from drippings. Let the meat cool 15 minutes. In a large soup pot, sauté carrots, onion, celery, and garlic in butter until onion is translucent, about 7 minutes. Add roasted oxtail and tomato paste. Deglaze the roasting pan with 1½ cups beef stock, removing all cooked bits and caramelized juices with a wooden spoon. Add pan juices and remaining beef stock to the pot. Add parsley, rosemary, and bay leaf and bring to a boil over high heat. Reduce heat to medium and cook at least 1½ hours until the meat slips off the bones. Remove bones from soup, if desired. Add potatoes and cook until tender, about 15 to 20 minutes. Turn heat to high and thicken soup with roux. Season with salt and pepper, to taste.

Serve with favorite artisan bread.

French Soup Pot

Makes 12 servings

3 pounds lean beef brisket
¼ pound salt pork
1 whole onion, pierced with 2 whole cloves
3 leeks, cut in chunks, or 1 bunch green onions, sliced in 1-inch lengths
8 ribs celery, cut in chunks
9 carrots, peeled and halved lengthwise, divided
1 turnip, peeled and cut in chunks
1 teaspoon thyme
Parsley, to taste
Water to cover ingredients
1 tablespoon salt
1 (3½–4 pound) whole chicken, legs and wings bound to body
6 potatoes, peeled
1 small head cabbage, cut in 6 pieces

Place brisket, pork, onion, leeks or green onions, celery, 6 carrot halves, turnip, thyme, and parsley in a large, heavy soup pot. Cover with water and bring to a boil. Add salt. Reduce heat and simmer, covered, for 1½ hours. Add chicken, cover, and cook 30 minutes more. Add potatoes, remaining carrots, and cabbage; cover and cook 30 minutes or until vegetables are tender.

Serve broth in soup dishes with meat and vegetables on plates on the side.

Minestrone

Makes 12 (1-cup) servings

- 1 cup navy beans
- ½ pound diced bacon
- ⅓ pound diced ham
- ½ cup chopped onion
- 2 cups beef stock
- 2 tablespoons Worcestershire sauce
- 1½ cups canned tomatoes, diced
- 1½ cups peeled, chopped carrots
- 1 cup cut green beans
- 2 cups coarsely chopped cabbage
- 1 cup chopped celery
- 1 cup small shell pasta or macaroni
- Salt and pepper, to taste

Soak beans overnight in enough water to cover. Drain, rinse, and drain again. Boil beans in fresh water until tender, about 2 hours; add more water as needed. Cook bacon until crisp; drain, and crumble. Sauté ham and onion in bacon fat. Add beef stock, Worcestershire sauce, bacon, ham, onion, tomatoes, carrots, green beans, cabbage, celery, and pasta to the beans. Cook until fresh vegetables are tender, 10 to 15 minutes. Add salt and pepper, to taste.

Chef's Tip: For quicker preparation use 2 (15-ounce) cans navy beans, drained and rinsed, in place of soaked navy beans.

Sausage Soup with Pinch Noodles

Makes 6 servings

- ½ pound dried pinto beans
- Water
- 2 tablespoons vegetable oil
- 1 small onion, chopped
- ½ pound smoked sausage
- 2 tablespoons flour
- 1½ teaspoons paprika
- 5 cups water
- 1 or 2 bay leaves
- 1 teaspoon salt
- 1 medium carrot, peeled and cut in thin, 3-inch-long strips
- 1 small parsnip, peeled and cut in thin, 3-inch-long strips
- 1½ teaspoons white vinegar
- ½ cup sour cream, plus more for garnish

Pinch Noodles

- ½ cup flour
- Pinch of salt
- 1 egg
- 1 teaspoon water, optional

Place beans in a colander and rinse well under cold running water. Drain beans, place in a medium bowl with enough water to cover them, and soak overnight.

The next day, drain beans in a colander and set aside. In a large soup pot, heat oil over medium heat; add onion and sausage and sauté until onion is translucent and sausage is browned. Add flour and cook, stirring constantly, until flour is light brown. Stir in beans, paprika, 5 cups water, bay leaves, salt, carrot, and parsnip. Cover and simmer over low to medium-low heat about 2 hours. Bring soup to a boil, add Pinch Noodles, and boil gently until noodles are tender. Reduce heat and continue simmering, if necessary, until beans are tender.

For noodles: Combine flour, salt, and egg in a medium bowl. Knead until stiff dough forms. Add 1 teaspoon water, if necessary. Flatten dough between your palms until it is about ⅛-inch thick. Pinch off ½-inch pieces of dough and drop into boiling soup.

Just before serving, stir in vinegar. Place 1 cup hot soup in a small bowl, add ½ cup sour cream, and stir until smooth. Add sour cream mixture to soup pot and stir well until heated through. Do not boil. Garnish individual servings with a dollop of sour cream.

Vegetable and Sausage Soup (shown on page 2)

Makes 6 servings

6 cups chicken broth
1 pound Polska kielbasa or smoked sausage, diced
3 or 4 medium potatoes, peeled and diced
1 (15-ounce) can kidney beans
1 (14½-ounce) can diced tomatoes, undrained
½ head green cabbage, coarsely chopped
1 medium onion, chopped
1 large carrot, peeled and diced
½ green bell pepper, diced
3 cloves garlic, minced
Salt and pepper, to taste

Combine chicken broth, sausage, potatoes, beans, tomatoes, cabbage, onion, carrot, bell pepper, and garlic in a large soup pot. Bring to a boil, stirring occasionally. Reduce heat; simmer, uncovered, until thick, stirring occasionally, about 2 hours. Season with salt and pepper, to taste. This soup is even better made a day ahead; cool and skim off all the fat before reheating.

Serve with toasted rye bread.

Slow Cooker: Using only 5 cups of chicken broth, place all ingredients in slow cooker. Cook on low 6 to 8 hours or on high 3 to 4 hours. Leave the lid on the cooker while cooking.

Country Bacon Soup

Makes 6 servings

1 tablespoon butter or margarine
½ cup chopped onion
7 slices bacon, fried, drained, and crumbled, reserving 2 slices for garnish
1 (10¾-ounce) can condensed cream of mushroom soup
1 (10½-ounce) can condensed vegetarian vegetable soup
1 (11½-ounce) can condensed bean with bacon soup
1 cup whole kernel corn (canned or frozen), drained
1¼ cups milk
¾ cup water
2 medium potatoes, cooked, peeled, and diced
Salt and pepper, to taste

Melt butter or margarine in a large, heavy saucepan over medium heat; add onion and sauté until clear. Stir in bacon, soups, corn, milk, water, and potatoes. Cook over medium heat, stirring frequently, until heated through. Season with salt and pepper, to taste.

To serve, ladle into bowls and garnish with crumbled bacon in the middle.

Slow Cooker: Brown bacon and crumble, reserving 2 strips for garnish. Place all ingredients in a slow cooker and cook on high 3 to 4 hours.

Gumbo Soup

Makes 12 to 16 servings

¼ cup butter
3 large yellow onions, diced
2 large red bell peppers, diced
1 stalk celery, diced
1 (14½-ounce) can diced tomatoes, undrained
1 (7-ounce) can diced green chiles, undrained
2 cups clam juice
1 cup tomato juice
4 cups water
1 (15-ounce) can black beans, rinsed
½ pound salad shrimp
¼ cup uncooked rice
½ pound pork sausage
½ teaspoon minced garlic
1 teaspoon cayenne pepper
2 tablespoons paprika
½ cup brown sugar
1½ teaspoons salt
3 cups frozen sliced okra

Melt butter in a large soup pot over medium-high heat. Add onions, peppers, and celery and sauté until tender. Stir in tomatoes and chiles. Add clam juice, tomato juice, and water; bring to a boil. Stir in beans, shrimp, and rice. Reduce to medium heat and simmer. While soup simmers, brown sausage in a medium skillet; drain off fat. Add sausage, garlic, cayenne pepper, paprika, brown sugar, salt, and okra to soup. Cook until rice is tender.

Slow Cooker: Place all ingredients in slow cooker and cook on high 3 to 4 hours or on low 6 to 8 hours.

Italian Sausage Vegetable Soup

Makes 8 servings

6 ounces Italian sausage
2 (14½-ounce) cans stewed tomatoes, undrained
2 cups beef broth
1 (10–12-ounce) package frozen mixed vegetables
½ teaspoon salt
½ teaspoon garlic powder
¾ cup uncooked small seashell pasta

Brown sausage in a large saucepan over medium heat, cooking and stirring until crumbly. Drain sausage and wipe drippings from pan with a paper towel. Return sausage to pan and stir in tomatoes, broth, vegetables, salt, and garlic powder. Bring to a boil. Cover, reduce heat to medium-low, and cook 5 minutes. Stir in pasta shells; cover and cook an additional 10 minutes or until pasta is tender.

Serve with Parmesan crostini (page 25).

Slow Cooker: Prepare sausage as above. Place all ingredients, except pasta, in slow cooker. Cook on high 2½ hours. Add pasta and cook an additional 30 to 40 minutes.

Peasant Soup

Makes 8 servings

- 1 cup great Northern beans
- 7 cups water, divided
- 1 teaspoon salt
- 1 ham hock (or ½ pound bacon or diced ham)
- 3 carrots, peeled and diced
- 1 onion, chopped
- 1 cup chopped celery
- 2 cups chopped cabbage, plus cabbage wedges for garnish
- ½ teaspoon garlic powder
- ½ teaspoon pepper
- 1 tablespoon taco seasoning

Cover beans with water and soak overnight (or bring to a boil for 2 minutes, remove from heat, and let stand, covered, 1 hour). Drain beans and combine with 3 cups water, salt, and ham hock in a large soup pot. Cover and simmer until beans are tender, about 2 hours. Add carrots, onion, celery, chopped cabbage, garlic powder, pepper, taco seasoning, and 4 cups water. Simmer, covered, until vegetables are tender. Remove ham hock and strip meat from bone. Dice meat and return to soup.

To serve, cut a cabbage wedge in half and slice thin wedges (½-inch wide on the long end), leaving a piece of the core attached. After ladling soup into bowls, place wedges on piping hot soup to soften them.

Chef's Tip: For easier preparation, substitute 2 (15-ounce) cans great Northern beans, undrained, and omit the first three cups of water.

Slow Cooker: Prepare beans as above. Place all ingredients in slow cooker. Cook on high 3 to 3½ hours.

Oatmeal Zucchini Soup

Makes 6 to 8 servings

5 tablespoons butter, divided
1 tablespoon minced onion
1 pinch dried thyme
1¼ pounds small zucchini, chopped, plus 1 zucchini, sliced, for garnish
½ cup quick-cooking oats
1 tablespoon Worcestershire sauce
2 cups heavy cream
2 cups milk
2 cups water
Salt, to taste

Melt butter in a large saucepan, add onion, and sauté 2 minutes or until onion is translucent. Add thyme and zucchini and sauté 4 minutes. Add oats and cook, stirring for 2 minutes. Add Worcestershire sauce, cream, milk, and water, stirring constantly. Cover and cook 15 minutes on low heat or until zucchini is tender. Season with salt, to taste.

Sauté sliced zucchini in 1 tablespoon butter, for garnish.

Cancun Tortilla Soup

Makes 8 to 10 servings

2 tablespoons paste-style chicken base or 1 tablespoon granulated soup base
4 cups diced canned tomatoes
½ cup butter
1 (7-ounce) can diced green chiles, undrained
3 cups diced onion
10 cups water
5 cups dried refried beans
2 cups crushed thick corn tortilla chips
1 tablespoon cumin
1 teaspoon garlic powder
⅔ cup diced green onions
⅔ cup fresh chopped cilantro
Tortilla chips, for garnish
Sour cream, for garnish

Combine chicken base, tomatoes, butter, chiles, and onion in a large soup pot. Cook until onion is translucent. Add water, beans, chips, cumin, and garlic powder. Heat until thickened and beans are soft, about 5 minutes. Add green onions and cilantro about 5 minutes before serving. Garnish with crisp tortilla chips and sour cream.

Cuban Vegetarian Soup

Makes 6 servings

2 pounds butternut squash
1 pound malanga root
2 medium carrots
2 cups reserved vegetable water
2 tablespoons butter
1 cup chopped onion
¼ cup chopped cilantro
3 cloves garlic, minced
½ teaspoon cumin
6 cups vegetable stock
Salt and pepper, to taste

Peel butternut squash, malanga root, and carrots and cut into 1-inch pieces. Place vegetables in a soup pot of boiling water and cook until soft. Drain water and reserve for later use. Melt butter in a large saucepan, add onion, and sauté 2 minutes or until onion is translucent. Add cilantro, garlic, and cumin; stir and allow to cook 2 minutes. Add vegetables, vegetable stock, and reserved water. (If it doesn't equal two cups, fill cup with regular water to make up the difference.) Place batches of mixture in a blender and process until smooth, taking care to fill the blender container only one-third full and to vent the lid. Return pureed mixture to pot and heat but do not boil. Add salt and pepper, to taste. Serve with tortilla chips or crackers.

Borscht

Makes 8 servings

4 large beets
6 cups water
4 cups chicken or beef stock, divided
Juice of 1 lemon
Sugar, to taste
Salt, to taste
¼ cup cornstarch
2 cups sour cream, divided
2 egg yolks
Chopped fresh parsley, for garnish
2 hardboiled eggs, diced, for garnish

Scrub beets clean and place with water in a large saucepan. Bring to a boil and cook beets until tender. Set beets aside for use at another time. Transfer 4 cups of beet water to another large saucepan and add 3½ cups chicken or beef stock. Bring to a boil and stir in lemon juice, sugar, and salt. Combine ½ cup cold stock and cornstarch in a separate bowl and stir until smooth. Stir into soup; cook and stir until thickened. Combine 1 cup sour cream and egg yolks in a separate bowl. Gradually stir 1 cup hot liquid into egg mixture. Then, stirring constantly, slowly add warmed egg mixture to hot liquid. Heat through (do not boil). Strain.

Serve hot or cold, garnished with 1 cup sour cream, parsley, and diced eggs.

Macaroni and Tomato Soup

Makes 10 to 12 (1-cup) servings

2 tablespoons butter or margarine
½ cup chopped onion
¼ cup diced green pepper
1 cup diced celery
1 (10¾-ounce) can condensed tomato soup
1 can water
1 (46-ounce) can tomato juice
4 ounces macaroni, cooked
Dash of pepper
½ teaspoon salt, or to taste
½ teaspoon basil
1 tablespoon sugar
1 to 2 bay leaves

Melt butter in a heavy saucepan; cook onion, green pepper, and celery until tender but not brown. Add remaining ingredients. Heat to boiling.

Split Pea Soup

Makes 10 to 12 (1-cup) servings

2 cups (1 pound) split peas
8 cups water
1 cup chopped onion
1 cup chopped ham, or meaty ham bone or hock
1 tablespoon salt
¼ teaspoon pepper
1 carrot, peeled and shredded

Combine peas, water, onion, ham, salt, and pepper in a large soup pot. Simmer 1½ to 2 hours, or to desired consistency. Garnish with shredded carrots.

Chef's Tip: Add 1 pound cocktail sausages before serving.

Slow Cooker: Place all ingredients in slow cooker and cook on high 3½ to 4 hours or on low 6 to 8 hours.

Western Tomato Soup

Makes about 8 (1-cup) servings

3 slices bacon, for garnish
½ cup finely chopped celery
3 tablespoons finely chopped onion
¼ cup finely chopped green pepper
3 tablespoons flour
2 cups milk
1 (10¾-ounce) can condensed tomato soup
1 (14½-ounce) can stewed tomatoes
1½ cups tomato juice
Salt and pepper, to taste

Fry bacon until crisp; crumble. Sauté celery, onion, and green pepper in bacon fat until tender and translucent but not browned. Add flour and cook 2 to 3 minutes. Combine milk and tomato soup in a 3-quart saucepan; heat and stir until smooth. Combine all ingredients except bacon with tomato soup mixture. Heat and stir until slightly thickened. Garnish with crumbled bacon.

French Onion Soup

Makes 4 servings

3 cups sliced onion
¼ cup butter
2 cups beef stock (or 2 cups water and 2 teaspoons beef soup base)
2 cups chicken stock (or 2 cups water and 2 teaspoons chicken soup base)
½ teaspoon thyme
1 teaspoon salt
¼ teaspoon pepper

Parmesan Toast Slices

1 loaf French bread
Butter, room temperature
Parmesan, Swiss, or favorite cheese, shredded

Sauté onion in melted butter in a medium saucepan over medium heat until dark golden brown (caramelized), but not burned. Add beef stock, chicken stock, thyme, salt, and pepper. Simmer 30 minutes. Ladle into bowls and top with Parmesan Toast Slices just before serving.

For toast slices: Slice French bread into thin slices and place on a large baking sheet. Spread each slice with softened butter. Sprinkle liberally with Parmesan cheese. Place slices under broiler and toast until light brown. Serve whole or sliced.

Carrot Apple Curry Soup

Makes 6 servings

1 tablespoon olive oil
12 carrots, peeled and chopped
1 medium onion, chopped
⅓ cup white wine vinegar
8 cups vegetable stock
5 apples (any kind), peeled and chopped
2 tablespoons ginger powder
1 tablespoon curry powder
Salt and pepper, to taste
12 dried apple slices, for garnish
½ cup shredded carrots, for garnish

Heat oil in a large soup pot over medium-high heat. Add carrots and onion and sauté until they are slightly brown. Once the vegetables are softened, add vinegar and vegetable stock to deglaze the pan. Simmer carrots and onion for 10 minutes. Add apples and more vegetable stock if needed so that the carrots, onion, and apples are slightly submerged. Add ginger and curry powders and simmer 45 minutes or until vegetables and apples are very soft. Blend with an immersion blender* and adjust the seasoning with salt and pepper.

To serve, garnish with dried apple slices and shredded carrot.

**In place of an immersion blender, a regular blender may be used, with caution. Fill the blender about one-third full so that the hot liquid does not splatter over. Be sure to vent the lid of the blender so that the steam inside does not build up pressure.*

Vegetarian Bean and Butternut Squash Soup

Makes 12 servings

1 medium butternut squash
1 small onion, diced
1 tablespoon vegetable oil
2 medium peeled, diced carrots
1 (15½-ounce) can garbanzo beans, drained
1 (15-ounce) can kidney beans, drained
1 (15-ounce) can black beans, drained
1 (14½-ounce) can diced tomatoes, undrained
1 tablespoon Italian seasoning
1 teaspoon ground cumin
1 teaspoon salt
1 teaspoon black pepper
5 cups water

Peel butternut squash and cut in half. Using a spoon, remove the seeds. Dice squash into small pieces and set aside. Sauté onion in oil in a heavy soup pan over medium heat until onion is translucent. Add carrots to pan with onion and steam 1 to 2 minutes. Add remaining ingredients. Bring soup to a boil, lower heat, and let simmer until all the ingredients are thoroughly cooked.

Black Bean Soup

Makes 4 servings

1 cup chopped onion
2 cloves garlic, minced
1 tablespoon vegetable oil
2 (15-ounce) cans black beans, drained, divided
½ cup water
1½ teaspoons cumin
1 drop hot pepper sauce
1 (14½-ounce) can stewed tomatoes, undrained and diced
1 (14½-ounce) can chicken broth
1 (4-ounce) can diced mild green chiles, undrained
1 tablespoon lemon juice
¼ cup plain yogurt, for garnish

Sauté onion and garlic in oil in a large, heavy saucepan over medium heat, until translucent. Add 1 cup beans and mash with a potato masher. Stir in remaining beans, water, cumin, hot pepper sauce, tomatoes, chicken broth, and chiles. Bring mixture to a boil. Reduce heat; cover and simmer 15 minutes to blend flavors. Remove soup from heat and add lemon juice. Ladle into bowls and top each with a dollop of yogurt.

Zucchini Soup

Makes 4 to 6 servings

3 cups (about 1 pound) sliced zucchini
½ cup water
1 tablespoon fresh or dried minced onion
1 teaspoon seasoning salt
½ teaspoon parsley flakes, or 2 tablespoons chopped fresh parsley
2 teaspoons paste-style chicken soup base, or 2 bouillon cubes, or 1 teaspoon granulated soup base, divided
2 tablespoons butter or margarine
2 tablespoons flour
⅛ teaspoon white pepper
1 cup milk
½ cup light cream
Paprika, for garnish
Sour cream, for garnish

Combine zucchini, water, onion, seasoning salt, parsley, and 1 teaspoon soup base in a medium soup pot. Cook until zucchini is tender and most of water has evaporated. Mash or puree zucchini and set aside. Melt butter in a saucepan; blend in flour and remaining soup base and pepper. Add milk and cream and simmer until thickened. Stir in pureed vegetables; thin with additional milk, if desired. Adjust seasonings to taste. Garnish with paprika and sour cream.

Golden Squash Soup

Makes 6 (1-cup) servings

1 small onion, sliced
2 tablespoons butter or margarine
¼ cup flour
5 cups milk
1½ cups peeled, cooked, and pureed winter squash (hubbard, banana, etc.)
1½ teaspoons salt
¼ teaspoon celery salt
⅛ teaspoon curry powder
Pepper, to taste
2 tablespoons chopped parsley, for garnish

Cook onion in butter in large saucepan until onion is translucent. Blend flour into butter and onion; add milk. Cook over low heat, stirring constantly, until thickened. Remove from heat; gently blend in squash, salt, celery salt, curry powder, and pepper. Heat to serving temperature but do not boil. Sprinkle each serving with parsley.

Chef's Tip: One (12-ounce) package of frozen pureed squash may be used in this recipe. After adding frozen squash, continue to heat soup only until squash is defrosted.

Canadian Cheese Soup

Makes 10 (1-cup) servings

½ cup chopped onion
½ cup butter or margarine
1 cup flour
⅓ cup cornstarch
½ teaspoon paprika
½ teaspoon salt
¼ teaspoon white pepper
4 cups half-and-half or milk, heated
4 cups chicken stock, heated
¾ cup peeled, diced carrots, cooked
¾ cup diced celery, cooked
1 cup shredded sharp cheddar cheese
⅓ cup chopped parsley

Sauté onion in melted butter until translucent but not brown, 5 to 10 minutes. Add flour, cornstarch, paprika, salt, and pepper. Cook about 10 minutes on low heat. Add half-and-half or milk and chicken stock; cook, stirring constantly, until thickened. Finely chop cooked vegetables, or mash slightly; add to milk mixture. Adjust seasonings to taste. Just before serving, stir in shredded cheese and chopped parsley.

Chef's Tip: Amounts of vegetables may be increased if thicker soup is desired.

Potato Soup

Makes 8 servings

1½ cups sliced leeks or green onions, plus more for garnish
2¼ cups water, divided
5 cups peeled, cubed potatoes
¾ cup chopped celery
1⅓ cups peeled, cubed carrots
2 teaspoons salt, divided
¼ cup butter or margarine
¼ cup flour
¼ teaspoon pepper
4 cups milk
2 cubes chicken bouillon

Slice leeks ⅛-inch thick and place them in a sinkful of cold water. Do not use the tough, dark green part. Vigorously stir leeks to remove grit. Place leeks in a colander and run cold water over them until there is no more grit in the water.

Sauté leeks or green onions in ¼ cup water in a large soup pot until tender. Add potatoes, celery, carrots, 1 teaspoon salt, and 2 cups water. Cover and simmer 20 to 25 minutes or until vegetables are tender.

Meanwhile, melt butter or margarine in a medium saucepan. Add flour, pepper, and 1 teaspoon salt. Cook until smooth and bubbly. Gradually add milk and bouillon. Cook and stir until mixture thickens. Stir into vegetables. Simmer, stirring occasionally, until heated through.

Garnish with sliced green onions.

Swiss Potato Soup

Makes 6 servings

2 tablespoons butter
¼ cup chopped onion
3 cubes chicken bouillon
1 pinch dried thyme
2 tablespoons all-purpose flour
1 cup milk
1 cup water
1 cup heavy cream
1 dash Worcestershire sauce
2 cups diced cooked potatoes
1 cup shredded Swiss cheese
Salt and pepper, to taste
Fresh herbs, to garnish

Melt butter in a large saucepan; add onion, bouillon, and thyme and cook over medium heat until onion is translucent. Add flour and cook 2 to 3 minutes. Add milk, water, cream, and Worcestershire sauce and mix well. Transfer soup to blender in small batches and process until smooth. (Fill blender only one-third full each time and be sure to vent the lid.) Return mixture to saucepan and add cooked potatoes and cheese. Add salt and pepper, to taste.

Garnish with your favorite fresh herb.

Potato and Leek Soup

Makes 5 servings

3 medium leeks
3 medium potatoes, peeled and sliced ⅛-inch thick
2 (14½-ounce) cans chicken broth
1¼ cups water
½ cup heavy cream (add up to ½ cup milk extra if you prefer a thinner soup)
2 tablespoons butter or margarine
2 teaspoons salt
¼ teaspoon pepper
Chopped chives, for garnish

Slice leeks ⅛-inch thick and place them in a sinkful of cold water. Do not use the tough, dark green part. Vigorously stir leeks to remove grit. Place leeks in a colander and run cold water over them until there is no more grit in the water.

Combine leeks, potatoes, chicken broth, and water in a large, heavy saucepan. Cover and bring to a boil over medium-high heat. Reduce heat and simmer 35 to 45 minutes or until vegetables are tender. Without draining off broth, mash vegetables in saucepan with a potato masher until they are fairly smooth. If they will not mash easily, soup has not cooked long enough. Simmer 10 to 15 minutes longer. Add cream (and milk, if desired), butter or margarine, salt, and pepper and heat soup just to the boiling point. (Do not boil.) Ladle into bowls and sprinkle each serving with chives.

Cream of Broccoli Soup with Cheddar Cheese

Makes 6 servings

4 tablespoons unsalted butter
½ cup chopped onion
½ cup peeled, chopped carrots
½ cup chopped celery
2 cloves garlic, minced
4 cups chopped broccoli
¼ cup all-purpose flour
4 cups heavy cream
1 cup chicken broth
1½ cups shredded cheddar cheese, divided
2 teaspoons Worcestershire sauce
Salt and pepper, to taste
Broccoli florets, steamed, for garnish

Melt butter in a large soup pot over medium heat. Add onion, carrots, celery, garlic, and broccoli and sauté until the vegetables are very soft. Add flour to the vegetables, making a roux. Pour in cream and chicken broth, mixing well. Simmer until mixture has thickened, about 4 minutes. Add 1 cup cheddar cheese and stir until cheese has melted into the soup. Season with Worcestershire sauce, salt, and pepper.

To serve, ladle into individual bowls and garnish with remaining ½ cup cheddar cheese and steamed broccoli florets.

Cream of Asparagus Soup

Makes 6 servings

¾ pound fresh or frozen asparagus, reserving 6 spears for garnish
1 cup salted water
3 tablespoons butter or margarine
¼ cup minced onion
3 tablespoons flour
1 (14½-ounce) can chicken broth
1 cup milk
¼ teaspoon paprika
½ teaspoon salt

Simmer asparagus in water, covered, until tender. Cool slightly and puree asparagus and water in blender; set aside.

In a heavy soup pot, melt butter or margarine over medium-high heat; add onion and sauté until soft. Stir in flour, making a roux. Add pureed asparagus, chicken broth, milk, paprika, and salt. Cook and stir until slightly thickened.

To garnish, slice reserved asparagus spears diagonally into ½-inch pieces, and place on individual servings of soup.

Chef's Tip: One (15-ounce) can asparagus, undrained, may be substituted for fresh asparagus. Puree and follow rest of directions.

Cream of Leek Soup

Makes 8 to 10 servings

- 4 cups chicken stock (or 4 cups water and 4 teaspoons chicken soup base)
- 3 large leeks (about 3 cups chopped), reserving ¼ cup for garnish
- 1 cup chopped celery
- 1 cup chopped onion
- 6 potatoes, cooked, peeled, and cubed, reserving ½ cup cooked peelings for garnish
- 1 bay leaf
- 1 teaspoon salt
- Black pepper, to taste
- 3 cups milk
- Roux to thicken (page 7)
- 1 cup vegetable oil

Heat chicken stock in large soup pot. Trim dark green tops from leeks at the point where they turn light green; discard tops. Coarsely chop leeks and wash thoroughly. Add leeks, celery, onion, potatoes, bay leaf, salt, and pepper to chicken stock and simmer until vegetables are tender. Stir in milk and heat through.

Make a roux in a separate saucepan. Add 3 tablespoons roux to soup and allow to come to a boil, stirring gently. Continue to add roux 2 tablespoons at a time, bringing to a boil and stirring gently after each addition, until soup reaches desired consistency.

Heat 1 cup oil and fry reserved leeks and potato peelings until crispy. Ladle soup into bowls and garnish with fried leeks and peelings.

Creamy Vegetable Soup

Makes 4 servings

3 tablespoons butter or margarine
1 large carrot, peeled and thinly sliced, plus ½ carrot, shredded, for garnish
1 medium onion, thinly sliced
1 large potato, peeled and thinly sliced
3 cloves garlic, crushed
1 bay leaf
¼ teaspoon thyme
2½ cups chicken broth, divided
2 cups whole milk
⅛ teaspoon salt
⅛ teaspoon black pepper

Melt butter or margarine in a heavy saucepan over low heat. Sauté carrot, onion, potato, garlic, bay leaf, and thyme for 1 minute. Stir in ½ cup chicken broth and cook, covered, until liquid has mostly evaporated, about 15 minutes. Stir in remaining 2 cups chicken broth and milk. Cook, uncovered, over medium heat, stirring occasionally, until vegetables are tender, about 30 minutes. Stir in salt and pepper.

Garnish with shredded carrots. Serve with bruschetta (see below).

Bruschetta

Bruschetta is a crostini topped with savory ingredients such as julianned, roasted red bell peppers; diced tomatoes and basil with fresh mozzarella; minced sautéed mushrooms, onions, and garlic; fresh pesto and a slice of sundried tomato; or any cheese at room temperature (return the crostini to the oven and bake the cheese in).

Creamy Butternut Squash Soup

Makes 6 servings

1 medium butternut squash
2 pounds baby carrots
1 cup butter, divided
¼ cup packed brown sugar
1½ teaspoon salt, divided
1 small white onion, roughly chopped
2 cloves garlic, minced
1 rib celery, roughly chopped
4 cups heavy cream
1 teaspoon sugar, to taste
Pinch cayenne pepper, optional
Pinch ground cloves, optional
Pinch cinnamon, optional
Sour cream, for garnish

Peel and cube butternut squash. Discard seeds. Steam baby carrots until soft.

Preheat oven to 350 degrees F. Melt ½ cup butter. Toss squash with melted butter and sprinkle with brown sugar and 1 teaspoon salt in a medium bowl. Spread on a baking sheet. Bake squash for 30 to 45 minutes or until soft and brown on top.

In a soup pot, melt remaining ½ cup butter and sauté onion, garlic, and celery until soft and translucent. Add previously steamed carrots and baked squash to the soup pot. Puree the mixture well with a hand immersion blender* and slowly add cream, sugar, ½ teaspoon salt, and spices, to taste. Simmer until it reaches desired consistency.

**In place of an immersion blender, a regular blender may be used. Fill the blender about one-third full so that the hot liquid does not splatter over. Vent the lid of the blender so that the steam inside does not build up pressure.*

Creamy Southwestern Chicken Soup

Makes 6 servings

2 tablespoons butter
2 tablespoons flour
2 cups heavy cream
3 cups milk
2 teaspoons taco seasoning
2 teaspoons paprika
1 chicken bouillon cube
2 chicken breasts, cooked and diced
1 (4-ounce) can diced green chiles
½ cup cooked rice
1 cup frozen corn
1 cup black beans
Chopped cilantro, for garnish

Make a roux by melting butter in a heavy soup pot over medium heat until butter is foamy. Mix in flour, stir, and cook 1½ to 2 minutes. Slowly add cream and milk. Mix in taco seasoning, paprika, and bouillon cube. Cook and stir until thickened. Add chicken, chiles, rice, corn, and beans. Warm through. Garnish with chopped cilantro.

Cream of Spinach and Mushroom Soup

Makes 8 servings

- 2 tablespoons butter
- ¼ cup diced yellow onion
- 2 cloves garlic, minced
- 3 cups sliced mushrooms
- 4 cups heavy cream
- 6 cups milk
- ½ cup water
- 5 tablespoons cornstarch
- 1 teaspoon salt
- 1 teaspoon white pepper
- 2 cups chopped fresh spinach

Garlic Croutons

- 6–8 slices bread
- 4 tablespoons melted butter or salad oil
- 2 teaspoons minced garlic
- 2 teaspoons Italian seasoning

Melt butter in a soup pot and sauté onion and garlic for 3 minutes. Add mushrooms and continue cooking while stirring with a whisk until mushrooms look soft, about 4 minutes. Add cream and milk. Stir over low heat until surface bubbles.

Mix water with cornstarch to make cornstarch slurry to thicken the soup. Add slurry, salt, pepper, and spinach to soup. To serve, ladle soup into bowls and top with homemade or purchased croutons.

For croutons: Cut bread into small cubes and put into a bowl. Add butter or salad oil, garlic, and Italian seasoning. Mix well and transfer to baking pan. Bake 8 to 12 minutes at 350 degrees F. or until golden brown.

Savory Tomato Basil Bisque (photo on front cover)

Makes 6 servings

8 medium ripe tomatoes
3 Roma tomatoes
4 tablespoons olive oil, divided
1 medium yellow onion, diced
2 tablespoons minced garlic
1 small bunch basil, stemmed and chopped
1 (14½-ounce) can vegetable broth
1 (12-ounce) can tomato paste
4 cups heavy cream
1 tablespoon Cholula hot sauce
Salt and pepper, to taste
2 tablespoons water
2 tablespoons cornstarch

Preheat oven to 350 degrees F. Remove stems from tomatoes and place tomatoes on a baking sheet. Coat generously with 2 tablespoons oil. Bake 10 minutes, or until peels come off easily. Set aside. Sauté onion, garlic, and basil in remaining 2 tablespoons oil in a large soup pot on medium heat. Add vegetable broth and simmer 5 minutes.

Peel baked tomatoes and add to pot. Puree with an immersion blender* until smooth. Add remaining ingredients to pot and season with salt and pepper as needed. If desired, thicken with cornstarch slurry of water and cornstarch mixed together. Boil to thicken.

Garnish with sour cream and serve with bruschetta (page 71).

**In place of an immersion blender, a regular blender may be used, with caution. Fill the blender about one-third full so that the hot liquid does not splatter over. Vent the lid of the blender so that the steam inside does not build up pressure.*

Lion House Tomato Bisque

Makes 10 to 12 servings

12 to 15 Roma tomatoes, reserving 1 roasted tomato for garnish
4 (10¾-ounce) cans condensed tomato soup
2 cups chicken stock
1 cup beef stock
1 (2½-ounce) bunch fresh basil, or 2 tablespoons dried basil
1 cup sugar, to taste
2 to 3 cups cream
Salt and pepper, to taste
1 cup sour cream, for garnish
2 tablespoons milk, for garnish

Place tomatoes on baking sheet and roast in oven at 350 degrees F. until tops blacken. Combine tomato soup, chicken stock, and beef stock in a large soup pot. Place roasted tomatoes and basil in blender and puree until smooth. Fill blender only one-third full and repeat until all tomatoes are pureed. Vent lid of blender so steam doesn't build up. Add puree to pot and simmer. Add sugar until mixture is slightly sweet. (Don't skimp on the sugar—it may take more or less, depending on the tomatoes.) Add cream. Season to taste with salt and pepper.

For garnish, stir sour cream and milk together until well blended. Place in a small zip-top bag and seal. Cut off a small corner of the bag and squeeze 8 to 12 small drops onto individual servings of soup. With a toothpick in the center of a drop, pull a line out, making it look similar to the picture at left. Continue with all drops of sour cream. Chop reserved tomato into fine pieces and place a few pieces in the center of each bowl.

Chef's Tip: The soup should not taste like marinara sauce but should have a slightly sweet, creamy flavor.

Shrimp Bisque

Makes 6 to 8 servings

2 tablespoons butter
1 teaspoon chopped garlic
½ cup diced yellow onion
1½ cups tomato puree
1 tablespoon Old Bay Seasoning
2 cups clam juice
4 cups heavy cream
1 teaspoon salt
2 cups cooked bay shrimp
Salt and pepper, to taste
3 chopped green onions, for garnish

Melt butter in a soup pot; add garlic and onion and sauté 3 minutes. Add tomato puree and Old Bay Seasoning; stir and cook 3 more minutes. When mixture starts to bubble, add clam juice, cream, and salt and return to a low boil to heat through. Since the shrimp is already cooked, add it at the last minute. Season with salt and pepper.

To serve, place in soup bowls and garnish with chopped green onions.

Seafood Bisque

Makes 6 servings

1½ to 2 cups cooked fish, such as halibut, salmon, or cod
½ cup cooked shrimp
¼ cup butter
½ cup diced celery
¼ cup minced green onion
3 tablespoons flour
2 cups milk
1 cup cream
1 cup fish stock or clam juice
1 teaspoon salt
4 drops red pepper sauce
⅛ teaspoon pepper
Minced parsley, for garnish

Shred fish and shrimp with fork and set aside. Melt butter in a heavy soup pot over medium-high heat. Add celery and onion and sauté until softened. Stir in flour. Gradually add milk, cream, and fish stock or clam juice. Cook and stir over medium heat until slightly thickened. Add shredded fish, salt, red pepper sauce, and pepper. Simmer a few minutes to blend flavors; do not boil.

Garnish each serving with minced parsley.

Carrot Bisque (shown on page 2)

Makes 4 servings

1 tablespoon butter or margarine
4 cups peeled, sliced carrots
1 cup diced onion
1 cup diced celery
1 cup diced parsnips, optional
Hot water to cover ingredients
2 cups half-and-half
½ teaspoon tarragon
Salt and white pepper, to taste
Chopped fresh parsley, for garnish

Melt butter or margarine in a large saucepan. Add carrots, onion, celery, and parsnips if desired; sauté vegetables briefly over low heat. Add enough water to barely cover the vegetables. Simmer until soft. Place one-third of mixture in a blender and puree until smooth, with lid vented. Continue processing vegetables until all mixture is smooth. Pour into large saucepan and add half-and-half, tarragon, salt, and white pepper. Heat through; do not boil.

Ladle into bowls, garnish with chopped parsley, and serve hot.

Carrot Apple Bisque

Makes 6 to 8 servings

5 to 6 large carrots, peeled
1 tablespoon butter or margarine
4 cups chicken broth, divided, plus more if needed
1 large apple, or ½ cup unsweetened applesauce
½ cup cream
½ teaspoon nutmeg
⅓ cup sliced green onion, including tops, for garnish

Cut carrots into ½-inch chunks. Combine in saucepan with butter and 1 cup chicken broth. Cook, covered, until carrots are very tender, about 20 minutes. In the meantime, peel, core, and slice apple, adding it (or applesauce) to carrots last 5 minutes of cooking. Remove pan from heat, uncover, and allow to cool about 10 minutes.

Place mixture in blender and process until smooth. Fill blender one-third full and repeat until all mixture is pureed. Vent lid of blender so steam doesn't build up pressure. Transfer to a soup pot.

Stir in cream, nutmeg, and remaining chicken broth. Additional broth may be added to reach desired consistency.

Serve hot, or cover and refrigerate to serve cold. Garnish with sliced green onion.

California Chowder

Makes 12 servings

½ cup butter
1 cup flour
1 tablespoon chicken soup base
2 cups heavy cream
4 cups milk
4 cups water
2 cups peeled, diced carrots
4 cups peeled, diced potatoes
2 cups diced celery
1 teaspoon granulated garlic, or 2 cloves fresh minced garlic
1 tablespoon salt
1 tablespoon Worcestershire sauce
1 cup finely chopped onion
1 tablespoon vegetable oil
2 cups fresh broccoli
2 cups fresh cauliflower
Fresh parsley or thyme, for garnish

Melt butter in a large soup pot. Add flour and mix well. Add chicken base, cream, milk, and water. Bring to a low boil and then add carrots, potatoes, celery, garlic, salt, and Worcestershire sauce. Cook 45 minutes. In a separate saucepan, sauté onion in oil for 3 minutes and add to soup with broccoli and cauliflower. Cook another 15 minutes or until vegetables are tender.

Garnish with fresh parsley or thyme.

Chef's Tip: Two (12-ounce) bags frozen California-blend vegetables, thawed and slightly chopped, may be substituted for carrots, cauliflower, and broccoli.

Chicken Corn Chowder

Makes 6 servings

- 2 slices bacon, for garnish
- ¼ cup chopped onion
- 3 tablespoons water
- 2 cups chicken broth
- 1 (10–12-ounce) package frozen whole kernel corn
- 2 potatoes, peeled and chopped
- ½ cup chopped celery
- ½ teaspoon salt
- ¼ teaspoon pepper
- 2 tablespoons flour
- 2 cups milk
- 2 cups chopped cooked chicken

Cook bacon until crisp in a large, heavy saucepan. Drain bacon, crumble, and set aside. Wipe drippings from saucepan with a paper towel.

In same saucepan, cook onion in water until tender. Add chicken broth, corn, potatoes, celery, salt, and pepper. Bring to a boil. Reduce heat; cover and simmer until vegetables are tender, about 15 minutes. Stir flour into milk until smooth. Pour into vegetable mixture and cook, stirring constantly, until thickened. Add chicken and stir 2 or 3 minutes more, until heated through.

Garnish with crumbled bacon.

Chef's Tip: For Southwestern flair, omit potatoes and add 1 red and 1 green bell pepper, diced. Garnish with chopped cilantro.

Vegetable-Cheese Chowder

Makes 8 to 10 servings

4 cups peeled, cubed potatoes
2 cups peeled, diced carrots
2 cups chopped celery
½ cup minced onion
2 teaspoons salt
4 cups water
1 (10-ounce) package frozen broccoli
2 tablespoons chicken soup base
3½ cups milk
½ cup butter or margarine
½ cup flour
1 tablespoon dry mustard
1 pound processed American cheese, cubed
1½ cups shredded cheddar cheese, for garnish
Cracked black pepper, for garnish

Place potatoes, carrots, celery, and onion in a large soup pot and add salt and water. Cook over medium-high heat until vegetables are tender, about 20 minutes. Stir in broccoli, chicken soup base, and milk. Simmer 5 more minutes. Make a roux in a separate saucepan by melting margarine over medium-high heat until foamy. Stir in flour and dry mustard and cook and stir until fragrant and golden brown, about 1 minute. Add roux to soup and stir until thickened. Add processed cheese to soup and stir until melted. Keep hot, without boiling, until ready to serve.

Garnish with shredded cheddar cheese and/or cracked black pepper.

Corn Chowder

Makes 4 servings

- 2 slices bacon, for garnish
- 1 small onion, chopped
- 1½ cups boiling water
- 1 (16-ounce) package frozen corn, or 1 (15¼-ounce) whole kernel can corn, undrained
- ½ teaspoon salt
- Dash pepper
- 1 (12-ounce) can evaporated milk
- 1 tablespoon butter
- 1 tablespoon flour

Cook bacon slowly in large saucepan until crisp; remove and drain on paper towels; crumble and set aside. Add onion to pan and cook until translucent but not brown, about 5 to 10 minutes. Add boiling water, corn, salt, pepper, and evaporated milk. Blend butter and flour to make a roux. Stir into soup mixture; mix until smooth. Cook until thickened.

Garnish with crumbled bacon.

Clam Chowder

Makes 6 to 8 servings

½ cup butter
½ cup finely chopped onion
½ cup flour
⅓ cup cornstarch
6 cups half-and-half or milk
3 (6½-ounce) cans chopped clams in clam juice, drained, reserving clam juice
1 cup peeled, diced potatoes, cooked
1 cup diced celery, cooked
1 teaspoon garlic salt
1 tablespoon Worcestershire sauce, optional
½ pound bacon, cooked and crumbled, optional
½ teaspoon dried thyme
1 teaspoon salt
½ teaspoon pepper
2–3 sprigs chopped parsley, for garnish

Melt butter in double boiler; add onion, and sauté. Add flour and cornstarch; cook 10 minutes. Add milk and reserved clam juice; cook until slightly thickened. Add clams, potatoes, celery, garlic salt, Worcestershire sauce, bacon, and thyme. Season with salt and pepper, to taste.

Serve in bread bowls and garnish with chopped parsley.

Salmon Chowder

Makes 6 to 8 servings

2 (8-ounce) salmon fillets, reserving ½ cup pieces, for garnish
1 teaspoon kosher salt, divided
¼ teaspoon ground black pepper
¼ cup butter
1 cup chopped onion
½ cup chopped celery
½ cup peeled, chopped carrots
3 tablespoons flour
3 cups milk
1 teaspoon thyme
½ teaspoon paprika
½ teaspoon Cholula hot sauce
1 teaspoon Worcestershire sauce
1 pound red potatoes, cut into ½-inch pieces
2 cups half-and-half
Lemon wedges, for garnish

Sprinkle salmon with ½ teaspoon kosher salt and pepper; place on a foil-lined baking sheet. Bake 15 minutes at 400 degrees F. or until desired degree of doneness. Break fish into approximately ½-inch pieces; set aside. Melt butter in a heavy soup pot over medium heat. Add onion, celery, and carrots and sauté 5 minutes or until tender. Add flour; stir until mixture is smooth. Gradually add milk, using a whisk. Cook over medium heat, stirring constantly, until thickened and bubbly. Stir in ½ teaspoon salt, thyme, paprika, Cholula sauce, and Worcestershire sauce. Add potatoes; reduce heat and simmer 20 minutes or until potatoes are tender. Add half-and-half. Cook 6 minutes or until heated. Add cooked salmon.

Garnish with reserved salmon and lemon wedge.

Bouillabaisse

Makes 8 servings

1 cup chopped onion
1 bulb fresh fennel, sliced ¼-inch thick and separated into rings
¼ cup yellow cornmeal
1 cup clam juice
2 (14½-ounce) cans chicken broth
1 (28-ounce) can Italian-style tomatoes
1 (6-ounce) can tomato paste
2 bay leaves
1 tablespoon basil
1 teaspoon finely chopped fresh garlic
½ teaspoon salt
½ teaspoon coarsely ground black pepper
2 tablespoons olive oil
2 tablespoons red wine vinegar
1 pound fresh or frozen raw shrimp
1 pound red snapper fillets, or any white-meat fish, skinned and cut into 1½-inch pieces
1 pound mussels in shells, scrubbed
Lime or lemon wedges, for garnish

Combine onion, fennel, cornmeal, clam juice, chicken broth, tomatoes, tomato paste, bay leaves, basil, garlic, salt, pepper, oil, and vinegar in a large soup pot. Place over medium heat and cook, stirring occasionally, for 1 to 1½ hours or until slightly thickened. While broth is cooking, peel and devein shrimp, leaving tails intact. Set aside. (If shrimp is frozen, do not thaw; peel under cold running water.) Add fish of choice and mussels in shells to broth mixture. Continue cooking, stirring occasionally, until fish separates easily with a fork and mussels open (10 to 15 minutes). Stir in shrimp and continue cooking until shrimp turn pink (4 to 6 minutes). Remove and discard bay leaves and any unopened mussels.

Ladle into bowls and garnish with lime or lemon wedges.

Vichyssoise

Makes 8 to 10 servings

4 cups chicken stock (or 4 cups water and 4 teaspoons chicken soup base)
3 large leeks (about 3 cups chopped)
1 cup chopped celery
1 cup chopped onion
6 potatoes, cooked, peeled, and cubed
1 bay leaf
1 teaspoon salt
Pepper, to taste
3 cups half-and-half
½ teaspoon nutmeg
¼ cup butter or margarine
½ cup flour
Unsweetened whipped cream, for garnish
Snipped chives, for garnish

Heat chicken stock in large soup pot. Trim tops from leeks where it turns from dark to light green; discard tops. Coarsely chop leeks and wash thoroughly. Add leeks, celery, onion, potatoes, bay leaf, salt, and pepper to chicken stock and simmer until vegetables are tender. Press cooked vegetables and chicken stock through a sieve. Return to pot. Stir in half-and-half and nutmeg and heat through. Make a roux in a separate saucepan by melting butter or margarine over medium-high heat until foamy. Stir in flour and cook until golden brown and fragrant. Add roux to soup and stir until thickened. Chill several hours.

Serve cold, garnished with unsweetened whipped cream and snipped chives.

Banana Bisque

Makes 6 servings

1½ cups whole milk
1½ cups heavy cream
4 bananas, sliced
¼ cup sugar
1 tablespoon vanilla extract
1 teaspoon molasses
Pinch of salt

Cinnamon Sugar Croutons

½ ciabatta loaf, cut into 1-inch cubes
6 tablespoons unsalted butter, melted
1 tablespoon sugar
1 tablespoon cinnamon

Put all soup ingredients together in a soup pot and blend with a hand immersion blender (a blender will work as well). Chill. Place 3 or 4 croutons in the bottom of each bowl. Pour ice-cold bisque over the croutons and garnish with a few more croutons on top. Serve immediately.

For croutons: Preheat oven to 400 degrees F. In a medium bowl, toss together bread cubes and melted butter. Stir sugar and cinnamon together until well mixed. Sprinkle on bread cubes and toss to coat. Arrange cubes on a baking sheet and bake until golden brown, about 8 minutes. Cool completely.

Gazpacho (shown on page 2)

Makes 8 servings

2 cups tomato juice
1 cup peeled, chopped tomatoes
½ cup chopped green bell pepper
½ cup chopped celery
½ cup chopped cucumber
¼ cup chopped onion
1 clove garlic, minced
2 teaspoons snipped fresh parsley
1 teaspoon snipped fresh chives
2 to 3 tablespoons vinegar
2 tablespoons olive oil
1 teaspoon salt
1 teaspoon cumin
½ teaspoon Worcestershire sauce
¼ teaspoon pepper

Combine all ingredients in a large bowl. Cover and chill in refrigerator at least 4 hours or overnight. Serve cold.

Chef's Tip: Three diced avocados may be added, if desired.

Salmon and Cucumber Soup

Makes 4 servings

Salsa

1 cucumber
1 tablespoon fresh chopped Italian parsley
1 tablespoon fresh lime juice
½ teaspoon salt
1 small red chile, seeded and finely chopped

Soup

2 medium cucumbers
1¼ cups strained plain yogurt
1 cup vegetable stock, chilled
¼ cup sour cream
1 tablespoon fresh chopped chervil, plus additional for garnish
1 tablespoon fresh chopped chives, plus additional for garnish
Salt and ground black pepper, to taste
1 tablespoon vegetable oil, for brushing
8 ounces salmon fillet, skinned and cut into 8 thin slices

For the salsa: Peel, halve, and seed cucumber. Dice into small pieces. Mix with parsley, lime juice, salt, and chile in a bowl. Stir to mix the flavors; cover and chill until needed.

For the soup: Peel 2 cucumbers and halve them lengthwise. Scoop out and discard the seeds. Roughly chop cucumbers and then puree in a food processor or blender. Add yogurt, stock, sour cream, chervil, chives, salt, and pepper and process until smooth. Pour mixture into a bowl, cover, and chill.

Brush a griddle or frying pan with oil and heat until very hot. Place salmon slices on griddle and sear them 1 to 2 minutes. Turn pieces over carefully and sear other side until tender and charred.

Ladle chilled soup into bowls. Top each with two pieces of salmon and a portion of the salsa in the center. Garnish with chervil or chives and serve.

Iced Melon Soup

Makes 6 to 8 servings

2 tablespoons sugar
½ cup water
10–10½ pounds very ripe melon, divided (cantaloupe and honeydew both work well)
Juice of 2 limes
2 tablespoons chopped fresh mint
3 tablespoons orange juice
2 tablespoons lemon juice
Mint leaves to garnish

For the sorbet: Place sugar and water in a pan and heat gently until the sugar dissolves. Bring to a boil and simmer 4 to 5 minutes. Remove from heat and allow to cool. Using half of the melons, cut each melon in half. Scrape out and discard the seeds and then scoop out the flesh. Puree in a food processor or blender with the cooled syrup and lime juice. Stir in the mint and pour the melon mixture into an ice-cream maker. Churn, following the manufacturer's instructions, until the sorbet is smooth and firm.

For the soup: Cut the remaining melons in half, scrape out and discard the seeds, and scoop out the flesh. Puree in a food processor or blender. Pour puree into a bowl and stir in orange and lemon juices. Place soup in refrigerator for 30 to 40 minutes, but do not chill it too long as this will dull the flavor.

Ladle soup into bowls and add a large scoop of sorbet. Garnish with mint leaves and serve at once.

Chef's Tip: If you don't have an ice-cream maker, follow these instructions. Pour melon mixture into a gallon-sized zip-top bag and lay the bag flat in the freezer until it is icy around the edges. Transfer to a food processor or blender and process until smooth. Repeat the freezing and processing two or three times or until the mixture is smooth and holding its shape. Then freeze until firm. For a color contrast between sorbet and the soup, use different color melons.

Turkey Dutch Oven Stew

Makes 6 to 8 servings

2 tablespoons vegetable oil
1½ pounds raw turkey (breast or thigh), cut into 1-inch cubes
1 large onion, chopped
4 medium potatoes, peeled and each cut into 12 to 16 pieces
4 carrots, peeled and sliced in ½-inch slices
4 ribs celery, sliced in ½-inch slices
1 teaspoon granulated garlic or 2 cloves minced garlic
1 tablespoon Italian seasoning
Water to cover the vegetables and meat in pan
2 (10¾-ounce) cans condensed golden mushroom soup
Salt, to taste
1 teaspoon coarse cracked black pepper

Heat oil in a large Dutch oven or soup pot until it is almost smoking. Add turkey and onion and cook until well browned. Add potatoes, carrots, celery, garlic, and Italian seasoning and enough water to cover them. Bring to a boil and then turn heat down to simmer and cook until the carrots are tender. Add mushroom soup, salt, and pepper and simmer 10 minutes.

Serve with a Lion House dinner roll (page 131).

Chef's Tip: Any cream soup can be used: cream of celery, cream of chicken, cream of mushroom. A favorite is golden mushroom.

Slow Cooker: Brown turkey in 2 or 3 batches in a very hot frying pan. Add the onions about halfway through the cooking process of the third batch. Browning meat in small batches allows the pan to stay hot enough to brown well. You will need 2 additional tablespoons oil for browning batches. Put all ingredients in slow cooker and cook on low 6 to 8 hours.

Creamy Chicken Leek Stew

Makes 8 servings

1 (2½–3 pound) broiler fryer chicken, cut up
4 cups water
½ cup peeled, chopped carrot
½ cup chopped celery
2 teaspoons salt
1 bay leaf
2 medium leeks, thinly sliced
1 small potato, peeled and diced
⅓ cup quick-cooking barley
2 cups light cream or milk
⅔ cup cut-up prunes, optional, divided

Rinse chicken pieces and place in a large saucepan with water, carrot, celery, salt, and bay leaf. Simmer about 25 minutes or until chicken is tender. Remove chicken pieces from broth. Skim off fat. When chicken is cool, skin and debone. Cut into bite-sized pieces and return to broth. Add leeks, potato, and barley. Simmer 15 to 20 minutes or until vegetables are tender. Stir in cream or milk. Add ⅓ cup prunes, if desired. Heat through and serve.

Use remaining prunes to garnish each serving.

Hearty Beef Stew

Makes 8 servings

1½ pounds lean boneless round steak
1 (14½-ounce) can stewed tomatoes, undrained and diced
3½ cups water, divided
1 medium onion, sliced thin
1 clove garlic, minced
1 teaspoon salt
¼ teaspoon pepper
1 bay leaf
1 tablespoon lemon juice
1 teaspoon Worcestershire sauce
6 carrots, peeled and cubed
4 potatoes, peeled and cubed
1 cup sliced celery
¼ cup flour

Prepare steak by trimming visible fat and cutting meat into 1-inch cubes. Coat a large soup pot with nonstick cooking spray and brown meat in pot over high heat. Add tomatoes, 3 cups water, onion, garlic, salt, pepper, bay leaf, lemon juice, and Worcestershire sauce. Heat to boil; reduce heat, cover, and simmer 2 hours, stirring occasionally to prevent meat from sticking to bottom. Add carrots, potatoes, and celery and cook, covered, an additional 30 to 35 minutes until meat and vegetables are tender. Blend ½ cup water with flour until smooth; pour gradually into stew and cook, stirring, until thickened, about 5 minutes. Remove and discard bay leaf.

Serve with toasted Italian-style bread or breadsticks.

Slow Cooker: Brown meat. Add all ingredients to cooker, but omit flour. Cook on high 3½ to 4 hours or until vegetables are tender.

Cowboy Stew

Makes 6 servings

- 1½ pounds ground beef
- ¾ cup chopped onion
- 1 teaspoon salt
- ¼ teaspoon pepper
- 1 (10¾-ounce) can condensed tomato soup
- 1 (10¾-ounce) can condensed cream of mushroom soup
- 1 (10¾-ounce) soup can of water
- 4 potatoes, peeled and cut into ½-inch cubes
- 4 carrots, peeled and sliced into ⅛-inch slices
- 3 ribs celery, diced

Brown ground beef and onion in a large frying pan. Add salt and pepper while meat is browning. When meat is done and onion is soft and translucent, transfer into a colander to drain excess fat. Return mixture to frying pan and add soups and water. Simmer 5 minutes. Arrange potatoes, carrots, and celery in a 9 x 13-inch baking pan. Pour meat and soup mixture over vegetables and stir. Cover with aluminum foil. Bake 1½ to 2 hours at 350 degrees F. or until vegetables are tender.

Serve with Sourdough Biscuits (page 129).

Chef's Tip: Serving yield can easily be increased by adding more vegetables, 1 can tomato soup, and ½ can water.

Slow Cooker: Brown ground beef and onion and drain off excess fat. Add remaining ingredients and cook on low 4 to 5 hours.

Brunswick Stew

Makes 10 to 12 servings

2 sweet onions, chopped
2 tablespoons butter
2 (14½-ounce) cans chicken broth
2½–3 cups water
2 (28-ounce) cans petite-cut tomatoes, undrained
⅔ cup ketchup
⅔ cup Worcestershire sauce
1½ teaspoons salt
½ teaspoon pepper
2 tablespoons Cholula hot sauce
1 pound pulled pork
3–4 medium potatoes, peeled and diced in ½-inch or smaller cubes
½ (22-ounce) bottle barbecue sauce (your favorite brand)
3 tablespoons white vinegar
1 (15-ounce) can peas
1 (15-ounce) can great Northern beans
1 (15-ounce) can navy beans
2 (14¾-ounce) cans cream-style corn

Sauté onion in butter in a 6-quart saucepan until onions are translucent. Add chicken broth, water, tomatoes, ketchup, Worcestershire sauce, salt, pepper, and hot sauce and bring to a boil. Simmer, uncovered, 1 hour, stirring occasionally. Stir in pork, potatoes, barbecue sauce, and vinegar. Cook 30 minutes on medium heat until potatoes are tender. Add peas and beans and simmer 20 minutes on low. Add corn and simmer until heated through.

This is delicious the day it's made, but it's even better a couple of days later.

Lamb Stew Pot

Makes 6 servings

- 5 slices bacon, cut into small pieces
- 1 onion, thinly sliced
- 1½ pounds boneless lamb stew meat
- 2 teaspoons salt, divided
- Flour
- ¾ cup water
- 4 teaspoons whole black peppercorns
- 1 large head cabbage
- 4 tomatoes, peeled and cut into wedges

Sauté bacon and onion in a large skillet until bacon is almost crisp and onion is tender. Transfer to a large soup pot, reserving drippings in skillet. Sprinkle stew meat with 1 teaspoon salt and dust with flour. Put meat into the skillet with reserved drippings and brown quickly on all sides. Add meat, water, and peppercorns to the soup pot. Cover and simmer 1 hour or until meat is tender. Remove meat from soup pot. Cut cabbage into 4 wedges and remove the core. Cut each wedge in half crosswise and break leaves apart. Arrange cabbage leaves, lamb, and tomato wedges in layers in the soup pot, sprinkling cabbage and tomato layers with 1 teaspoon salt. Begin and end with cabbage. Cover pot and cook gently 30 minutes more or until cabbage is tender.

This dish is traditionally served with hot boiled potatoes with melted butter and chopped parsley.

Pozole (Mexican Stew)

Makes 10 servings

2 pounds boneless pork loin, cut in 1 x 2-inch pieces
1 pound boneless pork butt, cut in 1 x 2-inch pieces
14 cups water
4 teaspoons salt
¾ cup diced onion
1 tablespoon dried oregano
1 sprig cilantro
3 cloves garlic, minced
2 (14½–16-ounce) cans hominy
Red sauce (see below)
1 tablespoon Cholula hot sauce, optional
Shredded cabbage, for garnish
Chopped onion, optional, for garnish
Lime or lemon wedges, optional, for garnish
Tostadas, for garnish

Red Sauce

10 chiles guerillas (dried chiles)
½ cup water
¼ onion
4 cloves garlic

Place pork in a large soup pot and cover with water. Add salt, onion, oregano, cilantro, and garlic and bring to a boil. As it boils, skim top layer of foam off surface of soup. Cook over medium heat until pork is tender, about 30 to 40 minutes. Do not cover with a lid while cooking. Add hominy, Red Sauce, and Cholula hot sauce, if desired, and cook another 15 minutes.

For the sauce: Boil chiles in water for 5 to 10 minutes. Transfer to a blender and puree with onion and garlic. Add to the Pozole.

Garnish with shredded cabbage, chopped onion, a wedge of lemon or lime, and tostadas.

Lion House Oyster Stew

Makes 6 servings

4½ tablespoons butter or margarine, divided
2½ tablespoons flour
2 cups milk
2 cups light cream
2 (8-ounce) cans oysters, undrained
½ teaspoon salt
¼ teaspoon black pepper

Make a roux by melting 2½ tablespoons butter in a heavy soup pot over medium-high heat until foamy. Stir in flour and cook until fragrant and golden brown. Reduce heat to medium. Gradually stir in milk and light cream, cooking and stirring until thickened. Add oysters, salt, and pepper. Heat slowly to simmer; do not boil.

When ready to serve, garnish with 1 teaspoon butter placed in the middle of each soup bowl and serve crackers on the side.

Lentil Stew

Makes 8 servings

- 1 cup dried lentils
- 4 cups beef broth
- 2 (14½-ounce) cans stewed tomatoes, undrained and diced
- 1 medium onion, chopped
- 2 ribs celery, diced
- 2 cloves garlic, minced
- 1 teaspoon rosemary
- ¼ teaspoon pepper
- 4 carrots, peeled and cubed, divided
- 2 tablespoons butter or margarine
- 8 small white boiling onions, peeled
- ¼ pound small fresh mushrooms, halved
- 4 potatoes (about 1 pound), peeled and cubed

Rinse and sort lentils and combine in a large soup pot with beef broth, tomatoes, onion, celery, garlic, rosemary, pepper, and half of the carrots. Bring mixture to simmer over medium heat. Cover and cook gently 30 to 35 minutes.

While mixture is simmering, melt butter in a large heavy skillet. Sauté the remaining carrots along with white onions until lightly browned, about 5 to 7 minutes. Stir in mushrooms and cook an additional 2 to 3 minutes, stirring constantly. Add potatoes and sautéed vegetables to soup in soup pot. Cover and simmer an additional 20 to 25 minutes or until potatoes and lentils are tender.

Calico Beef and Bean Bake

Makes 8 servings

½ to 1 pound ground beef
¾ pound bacon, cut in pieces
1 cup chopped onion
2 (15-ounce) cans pork and beans
1 (15-ounce) can dark red kidney beans, drained
1 (15-ounce) can butter beans
1 cup ketchup
¼ cup packed brown sugar
3 tablespoons white vinegar
1 teaspoon salt
Pepper, to taste
Sliced green onions, for garnish

Preheat oven to 325 degrees F. Brown ground beef, bacon, and onion in a 12-inch skillet; drain off fat. Transfer meat mixture to a 3 to 4-quart baking dish or 9 x 13-inch baking pan. Stir in remaining ingredients. Bake 1½ hours.

When ready to serve, garnish with sliced green onions.

Slow Cooker: Brown ground beef, bacon, and onion. Drain off fat. Add all ingredients to a slow cooker and cook on low 4 to 6 hours.

Hearty Chili

Makes 8 servings

1–2 pounds beef, diced (use your favorite leftover roast)
2 large onions, chopped
½ teaspoon cayenne pepper
1–2 tablespoons chili powder
1 tablespoon cumin
Salt and pepper, to taste
1 large green bell pepper, chopped
1 large red bell pepper, chopped
1 (12-ounce) bottle chili sauce
4 cups diced tomatoes
1 cup packed brown sugar
2 (15-ounce) cans red kidney beans, drained and rinsed

Brown beef and onions in a large heavy soup pot with cayenne pepper, chili powder, cumin, salt, and pepper. Add bell peppers and cook slightly. Add chili sauce, tomatoes, and brown sugar. Simmer 30 minutes on low and then add beans and bring to a low simmer again. Adjust seasonings.

Serve with scones made from Lion House roll dough (page 131).

Slow Cooker: Brown beef and onions. Place all ingredients in slow cooker. Cook on high 3½ to 4 hours, stirring once or twice during that time.

Vegetarian Chili

Makes 4 servings

1 cup chopped onion
3 cloves garlic, minced
1 cup water
½ cup diced green bell pepper
2 (14½-ounce) cans stewed tomatoes, undrained and diced
1 (15-ounce) can red kidney beans, drained
1 (15-ounce) can garbanzo beans, drained
2 tablespoons chili powder
1½ teaspoons cumin
¼ cup sour cream, for garnish

Spray a large soup pot with nonstick cooking spray and preheat it on the stove. Sauté onion and garlic in heated pot over medium heat for 5 minutes. Stir in water, green pepper, tomatoes, beans, chili powder, and cumin. Bring to a boil. Reduce heat and simmer 30 minutes, uncovered, to blend flavors and thicken chili.

Ladle into individual bowls and top each serving with a dollop of sour cream.

Slow Cooker: Place all ingredients, except sour cream, in slow cooker. Cook on high 3 to 4 hours.

Bread Bowls

Makes 6 bread bowls or 2 loaves French bread

½ cup warm water
2 tablespoons yeast
3 tablespoons sugar, divided
2 cups hot water
2 tablespoons salt
½ cup vegetable oil
5 cups all-purpose or bread flour, divided
1 egg white
1 tablespoon water

Preheat oven to 400 degrees F. Grease two 12 x 18-inch baking sheets and set aside.

Place warm water in a small bowl, sprinkle yeast on top, and stir in 1 tablespoon sugar; set aside. Place hot water, salt, 2 tablespoons sugar, and oil in a large bowl. Add 3 cups flour. Blend well. Add yeast mixture, stir well. Add the remaining 2 cups flour and stir well. Leave spoon in dough and let rise 10 minutes. Stir down and repeat 5 times.

For bowls: Divide dough into 6 equal pieces. Form bowl by slightly pulling top of dough toward the bottom and tucking it in until a round ball is formed. (It will be slightly flat where you have tucked the dough in.) Place bottom of dough on a greased baking sheet. Three bowls will fit on one sheet. Repeat with rest of dough. Whisk egg white and 1 tablespoon water together. Make 2 diagonal slits about ½-inch deep in the top of each bowl and brush with egg white mixture. Allow to rise 30 minutes. Place pan in oven. Squirt 5 sprays of water from a spray bottle into the oven. Bake 20 to 25 minutes. Cool completely. Cut the top off each bowl and remove most of the inside bread. Set to the side. To serve, ladle soup into bowl, set lid ajar over soup, and place scooped bread to the side.

For French loaves: Divide into 2 equal balls. Place one on a floured surface and roll out until it forms a rectangle 12 x 14 inches. Roll up like a jelly roll so you have a long loaf. Place on a greased baking sheet. Repeat with the remaining ball. Both loaves should fit on the same sheet. Make 3 diagonal slits about ½ inch deep on the top of the loaves. Brush with the egg white wash (see above). Allow to rise 30 minutes. Place pan in the oven. Before baking, squirt 5 sprays of water with a spray bottle into the oven. Bake 20 to 25 minutes.

Rich Corn Bread

Makes 9 pieces

1 cup all-purpose flour
1 cup yellow cornmeal
1 teaspoon salt
4 teaspoons baking powder
4 eggs
½ cup sour cream
1 (14¾-ounce) can cream-style corn
2 tablespoons vegetable oil
1 cup shredded cheddar cheese

Preheat oven to 400 degrees F. Grease an 8 x 4-inch loaf pan or an 8 x 8-inch square pan and set aside. Sift together flour, cornmeal, salt, and baking powder and set aside. Beat eggs until light. Add sour cream, corn, and oil to eggs. Stir in dry ingredients and beat well. Pour into prepared pan and sprinkle with shredded cheese. Bake 30 minutes. Test for doneness by sticking a toothpick into the loaf or pan, just off center. If the toothpick comes out clean, the bread is done.

Chef's Tip: If you like a little heat to your corn bread, stem, seed, and chop half of a jalepeño pepper and it to the batter before pouring into the pan.

Bread Sticks

Makes 24–36

2 cups warm water
1½ tablespoons dry yeast
4 tablespoons sugar, divided
1 tablespoon salt
¾ cup butter or margarine
5½–6½ cups all-purpose flour, divided
1 tablespoon vetetable oil
1–2 cups grated cheese: Parmesan, asiago, Swiss, cheddar or a mixture of your favorite flavors
Oregano or Italian seasoning, optional, for added flavor

Place water in large mixing bowl. Sprinkle yeast and 2 tablespoons sugar over the water. Stir to dissolve. Add salt, remaining sugar, butter, and half of the flour. Mix on low speed until smooth. Add remaining flour by ½ cup, mixing after each addition. Dough should be soft but not sticky. Remove dough from bowl and brush bowl with oil (so the dough doesn't stick or dry out). Cover bowl loosely with plastic wrap and allow dough to rise until double in size, about 45 minutes.

Place dough on floured surface and cut into two equal pieces; set one aside. Roll out half of dough to an 18 x 13-inch rectangle, about ½ inch thick. With a sharp knife or pizza wheel, cut 1-inch strips lengthwise and then cut them in half, making 9 x 13-inch breadsticks. Place strips on a greased or parchment-lined baking pan, leaving 1 inch between each piece. Repeat with reserved dough. Spritz dough strips lightly with water and sprinkle with grated cheese. Let rise 20 minutes and bake 15 minutes at 400 degrees F. Sprinkle with oregano or any Italian seasoning, if desired. Serve hot or at room temperature. They are best if eaten the day they are made.

Focaccia (Italian Flat Bread)

Makes 18 rolls or one 12 x 18-inch sheet pan

2 cups warm water
5¾ cups bread flour
2 teaspoons salt
¼ cup olive oil, plus a little more for brushing on bread
½ teaspoon garlic powder
¾ teaspoon oregano
1 tablespoon yeast

Place water in mixing bowl. Add flour, salt, oil, garlic powder, and oregano. Mix on low speed 30 to 45 seconds. Sprinkle yeast onto mixture and mix an additional 30 seconds. Mix 5 to 6 minutes on medium speed. Oil the top of dough and allow to double in size. Divide dough into 18 pieces for rolls and form into balls or make one ball for a sheet pan of bread. Brush with oil and allow to rest 30 minutes. Press out each ball by hand or spread the large ball onto a greased baking pan until it is very thin, like pizza crust. Brush top with oil and season as desired. Allow to rest 10 to 15 minutes. Bake 14 to 16 minutes in a preheated 450-degree F. oven or until lightly browned. Serve warm.

Parmesan Bread

Makes 1 loaf or 6 servings

2 tablespoons active dry yeast
2 cups warm water
2 tablespoons sugar
2 tablespoons butter, softened
2 teaspoons salt
½ cup grated Parmesan cheese, divided
3½ cups plus 2 tablespoons all-purpose flour, divided

Sprinkle yeast over water in a large bowl. Let stand 3 to 4 minutes and stir to dissolve. Add sugar, butter, salt, all but 1 tablespoon Parmesan cheese, and 3 cups flour. Beat at low speed until smooth. Beat in remaining flour. Cover bowl and let rise 45 minutes. Stir bread down; beat 25 strokes with a wooden spoon. Pour into a greased, 2-quart ovenproof bowl and sprinkle with reserved Parmesan cheese. Bake 45 to 55 minutes at 375 degrees F., or until nicely browned.

Dilly Casserole Bread

Makes 1 round loaf

- 1 package (2¼ teaspoons) active dry yeast
- ¼ cup lukewarm water
- 1 cup cottage cheese, heated to lukewarm
- 2 tablespoons sugar
- 2 tablespoons finely chopped onion or 1 tablespoon dried minced onion
- 1 tablespoon butter or margarine, softened, plus additional butter for brushing hot bread
- 1 tablespoon dill weed
- 1 teaspoon salt
- ¼ teaspoon baking soda
- 1 egg
- 2–2½ cups all-purpose flour

Soften yeast in water in a small bowl and set aside. In a mixing bowl, combine cottage cheese, sugar, onion, 1 tablespoon butter, dill weed, salt, baking soda, egg, and softened yeast. Add flour ½ cup at a time, to form a stiff dough, beating well after each addition. Cover and let rise in a warm place, until light and doubled in size, about 50 to 60 minutes. Punch dough down. Turn into a well-greased, 1½- to 2-quart round casserole dish. Cover and let rise in a warm place 30 to 40 minutes. Bake 40 to 50 minutes at 350 degrees F., or until golden brown. Brush with softened butter and sprinkle with salt.

Easy Cheesy Drop Biscuits

Makes 12 biscuits

- 1¾ cups all-purpose flour
- 2 tablespoons sugar
- 2½ teaspoons baking powder
- 1 teaspoon salt
- 1 cup shredded sharp or medium cheddar cheese
- 1 egg, beaten
- ¾ cup milk
- ⅓ cup vegetable oil

Preheat oven to 400 degrees F. Lightly grease a jelly roll pan or line it with parchment paper.

Mix together flour, sugar, baking powder, salt, and cheese in a large bowl. Beat together egg, milk, and oil in another bowl. Add to dry ingredients all at once, stirring with a fork until just moistened. Spoon by heaping tablespoons onto prepared pan. Bake 15 to 20 minutes.

Chef's Tip: This can also be baked as a loaf by greasing a 9 x 5-inch bread pan and pouring the batter into the pan. Bake 30 to 35 minutes or until a toothpick inserted into the center of the loaf comes out clean.

Sourdough Biscuits

Makes 36 biscuits

1 tablespoon yeast
1 cup warm water
6 cups all-purpose flour
2 teaspoons salt
¼ cup sugar
4 teaspoons baking powder
¼ teaspoon baking soda
¾ cup vegetable oil
2 cups buttermilk

Preheat oven to 400 degrees F. Dissolve yeast in warm water and set aside. Combine flour, salt, sugar, baking powder, and baking soda in a large bowl with a lid. Stir until well mixed. Add oil, buttermilk, and yeast mixture. Stir together until well mixed. Cover with a tight-fitting lid. Refrigerate 2 days. When ready to use, take out the desired amount and roll out, about ¾-inch thick, on a lightly floured board. Cut to desired size. Place on a well-greased baking pan and bake 10 to 12 minutes or until a light golden brown.

Chef's Tip: For optimal rising, do not open the oven door to check biscuits until the last 3 minutes of baking time.

Lion House Dinner Rolls

Makes 1½ to 3 dozen rolls, depending on shape and size of rolls

- 2 cups warm water (110 to 115 degrees)
- ⅔ cup nonfat dry milk
- 2 tablespoons active dry yeast
- ¼ cup sugar
- 2 teaspoons salt
- ⅓ plus ½ cup butter, margarine, or shortening, divided
- 1 egg
- 4½ to 5 cups all-purpose or bread flour, divided
- 1 tablespoon vegetable oil

Combine water and dry milk powder in a large bowl of an electric mixer, stirring until milk dissolves. Add yeast and then sugar, salt, ⅓ cup butter, egg, and 2 cups flour. Mix on low speed until ingredients are wet. Increase mixer speed to medium and mix for 2 minutes. Add 2 cups flour; mix on low speed until ingredients are wet and then for 2 minutes at medium speed. (Dough will be getting stiff, and remaining flour may need to be mixed in by hand.) Add remaining flour, ½ cup at a time, until dough is soft, not overly sticky, and not stiff. (It is not necessary to use the entire amount of flour.)

Remove dough off sides of bowl and pour oil all around sides of bowl. Turn dough over in bowl so it is covered with oil. Cover with plastic wrap and allow to rise in a warm place until doubled in size, about 1½ hours. Lightly sprinkle cutting board or counter with flour and place dough on floured surface. Roll out and shape as desired. Place on greased or parchment-lined baking pans. Cover lightly with plastic wrap. Let rise in a warm place until rolls are doubled in size, about 1 to 1½ hours.

Bake 15 to 20 minutes at 375 degrees F., or until golden brown. Melt ½ cup butter and brush rolls with melted butter while hot.

Chef's Tip: To freeze shaped rolls for later use, simply double the amount of yeast used when making dough. After the first rise, shape rolls but do not allow to rise again. Place rolls on a baking sheet and immediately place in freezer. When dough is frozen solid, remove rolls from pan and place in a plastic bag, squeeze excess air out of bag, and seal. Rolls may be frozen for 3 weeks.

When ready to use, place frozen rolls on greased or parchment-lined baking sheet, all facing the same direction. Cover lightly with plastic wrap and let thaw and rise until doubled in size, 4 to 5 hours. Bake as above.

Angel Biscuits

Makes 18 biscuits

- 1 package (2¼ teaspoons) active dry yeast
- ¼ cup warm water
- 5 cups all-purpose flour
- 1 teaspoon salt
- ¼ cup sugar
- 2 teaspoons baking powder
- 1 cup shortening
- 2 cups buttermilk
- 3 tablespoons butter, melted

Preheat oven to 400 degrees F. and grease a baking sheet.

Dissolve yeast in warm water and set aside. Stir together flour, salt, sugar, and baking powder. Cut in shortening with a pastry cutter or two knives. Add yeast to the buttermilk, and then add to mixture. Mix well with a fork, wooden spoon, or your hands. Turn dough onto a floured surface and pat to desired thickness. Cut biscuits with a round biscuit cutter or a glass cup. Dip biscuits in melted butter and place on greased pan. Bake 12 minutes, or until golden brown on top.

Chef's Tip: You may bake these immediately or leave out 30 to 40 minutes before baking. They may also be frozen, unbaked, if covered with plastic wrap and then foil. To use, remove from freezer and allow to thaw completely. Remove plastic and foil and bake as instructed above.

INDEX

Numbers in bold refer to pages on which photographs appear.